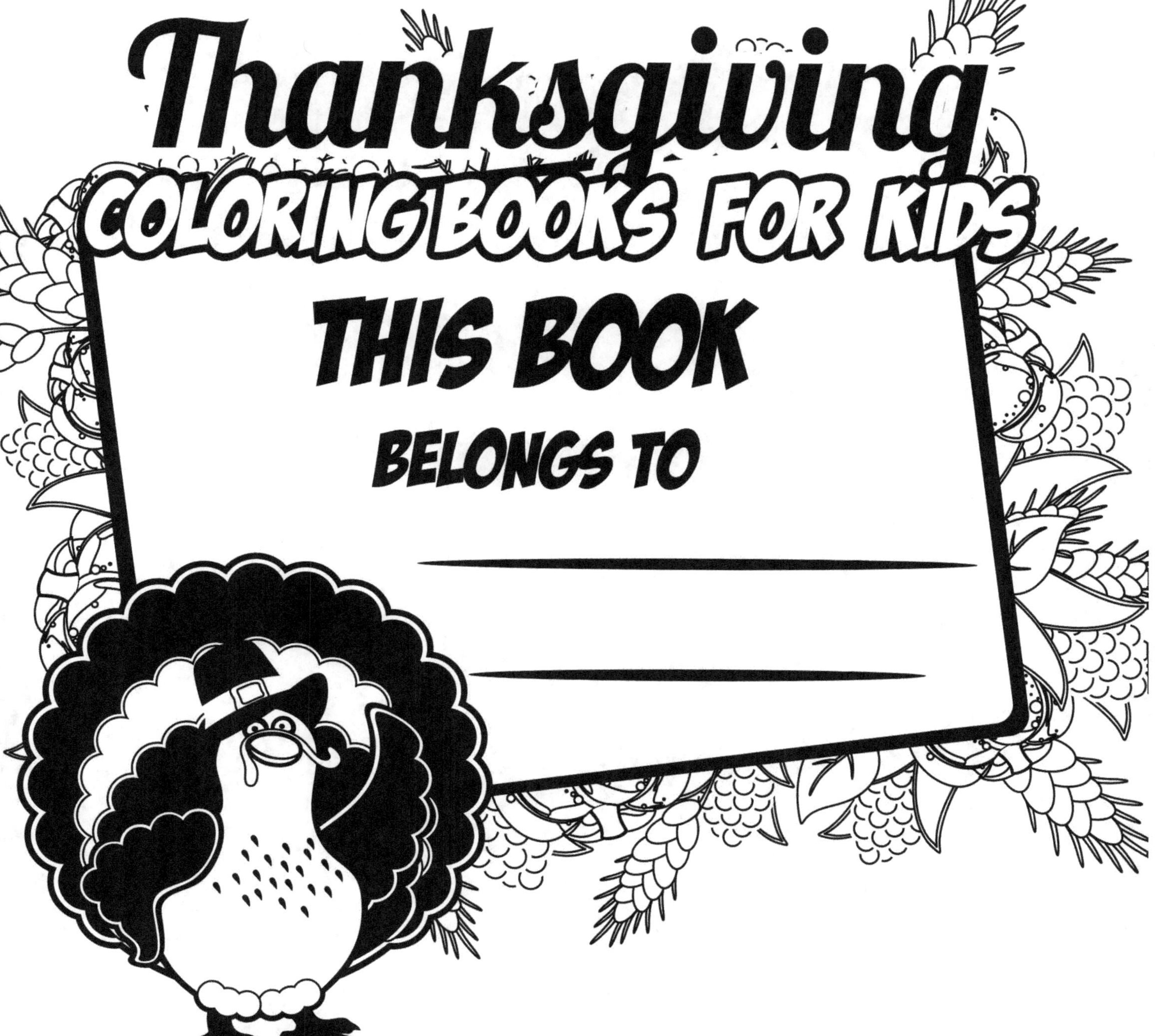
Thanksgiving
COLORING BOOKS FOR KIDS
THIS BOOK
BELONGS TO

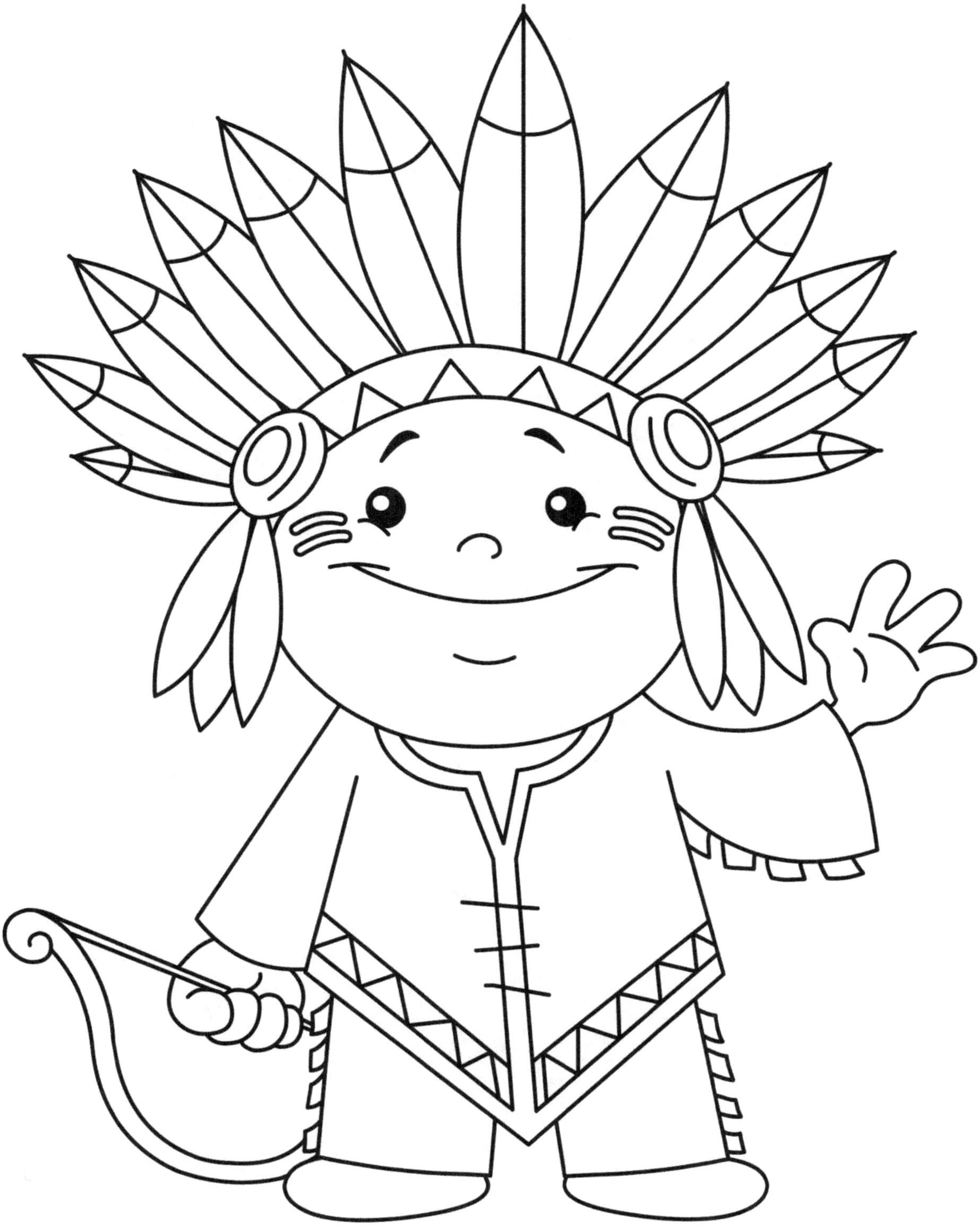

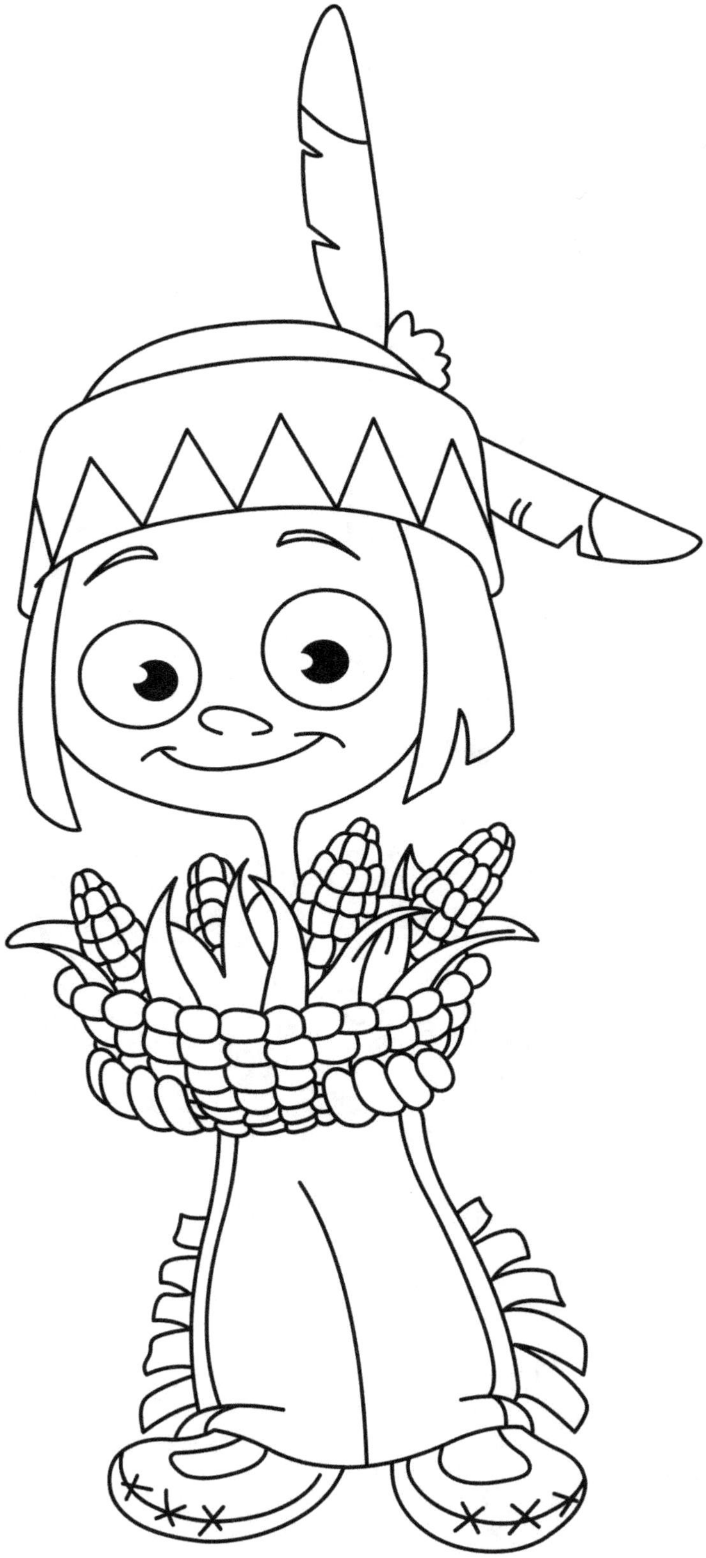

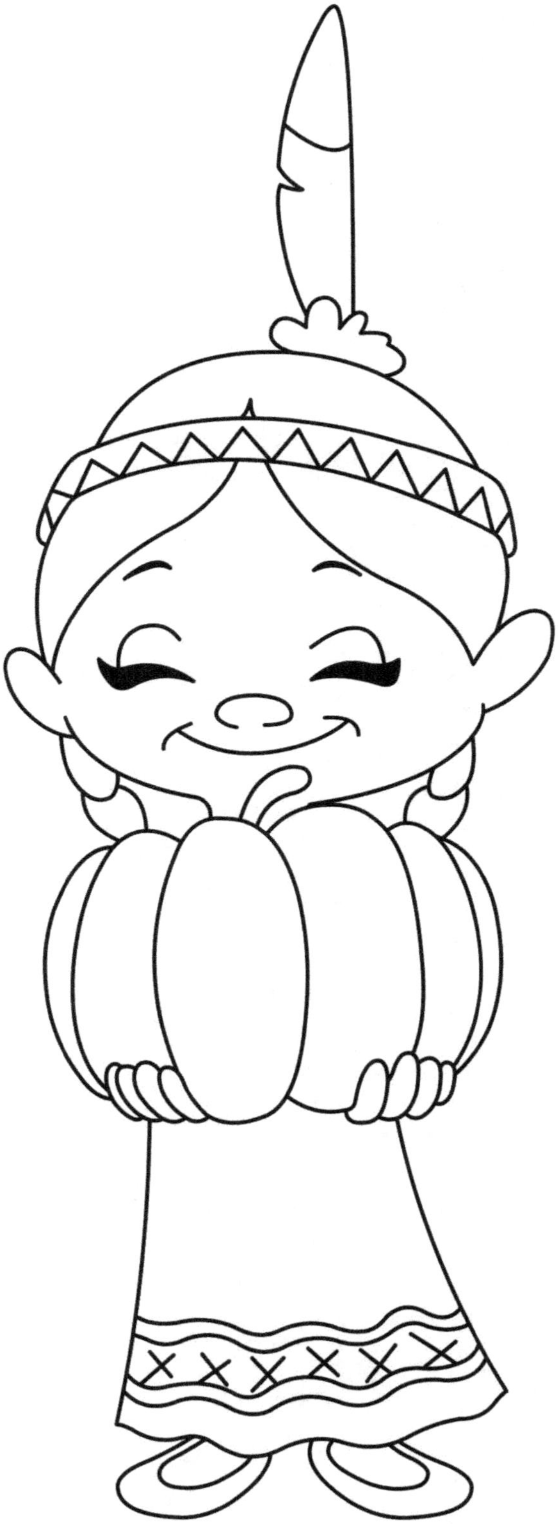

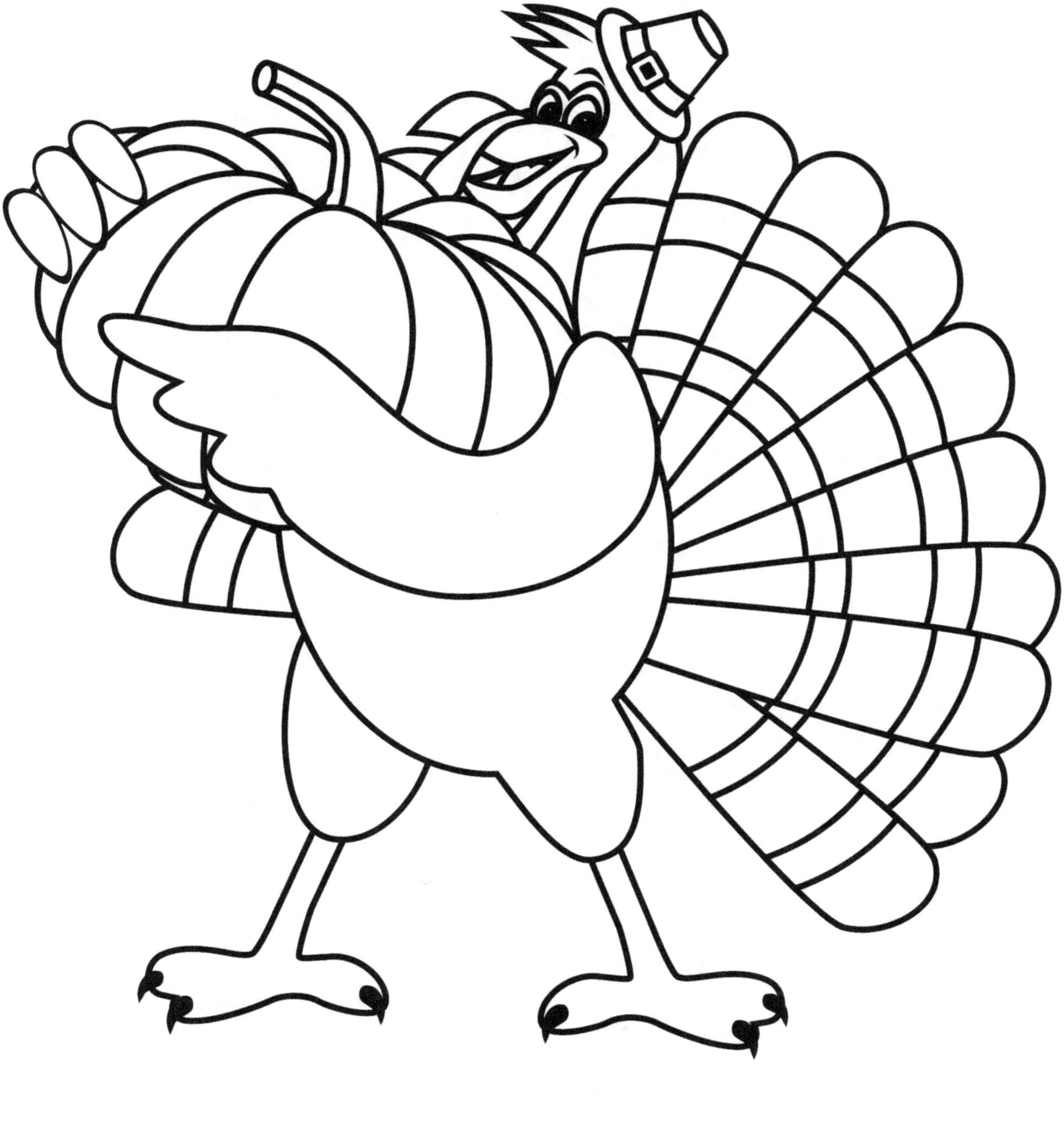

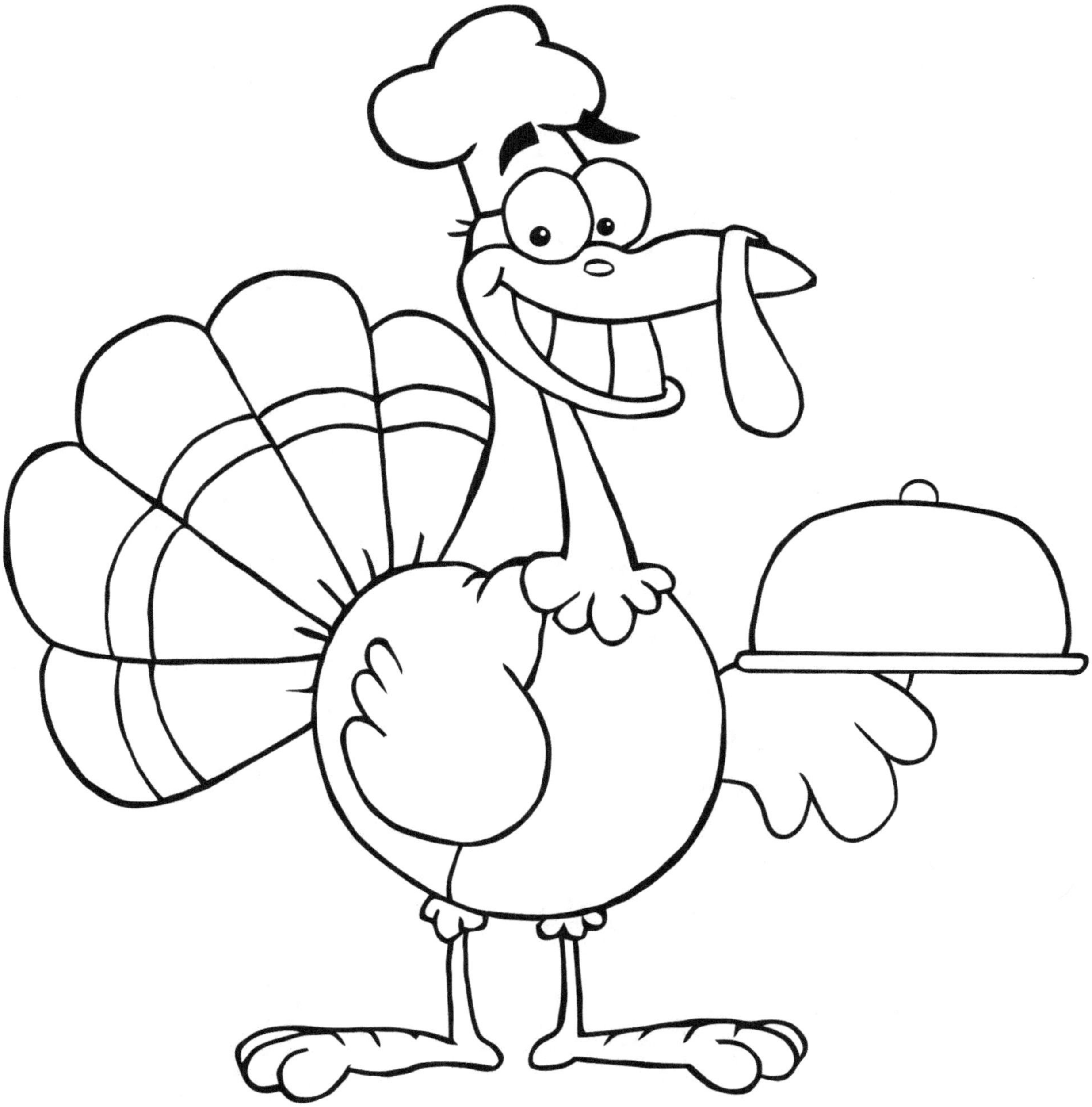

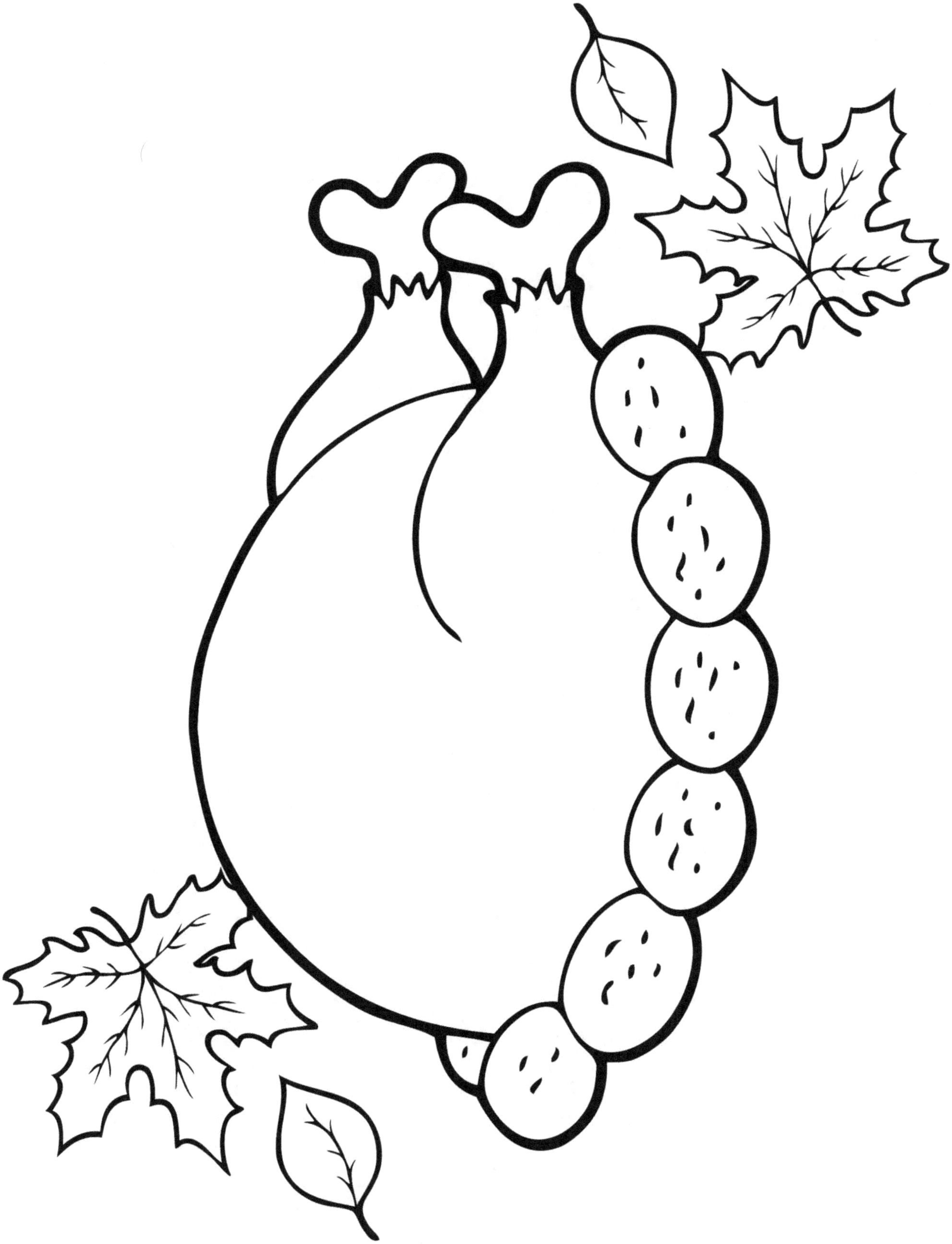

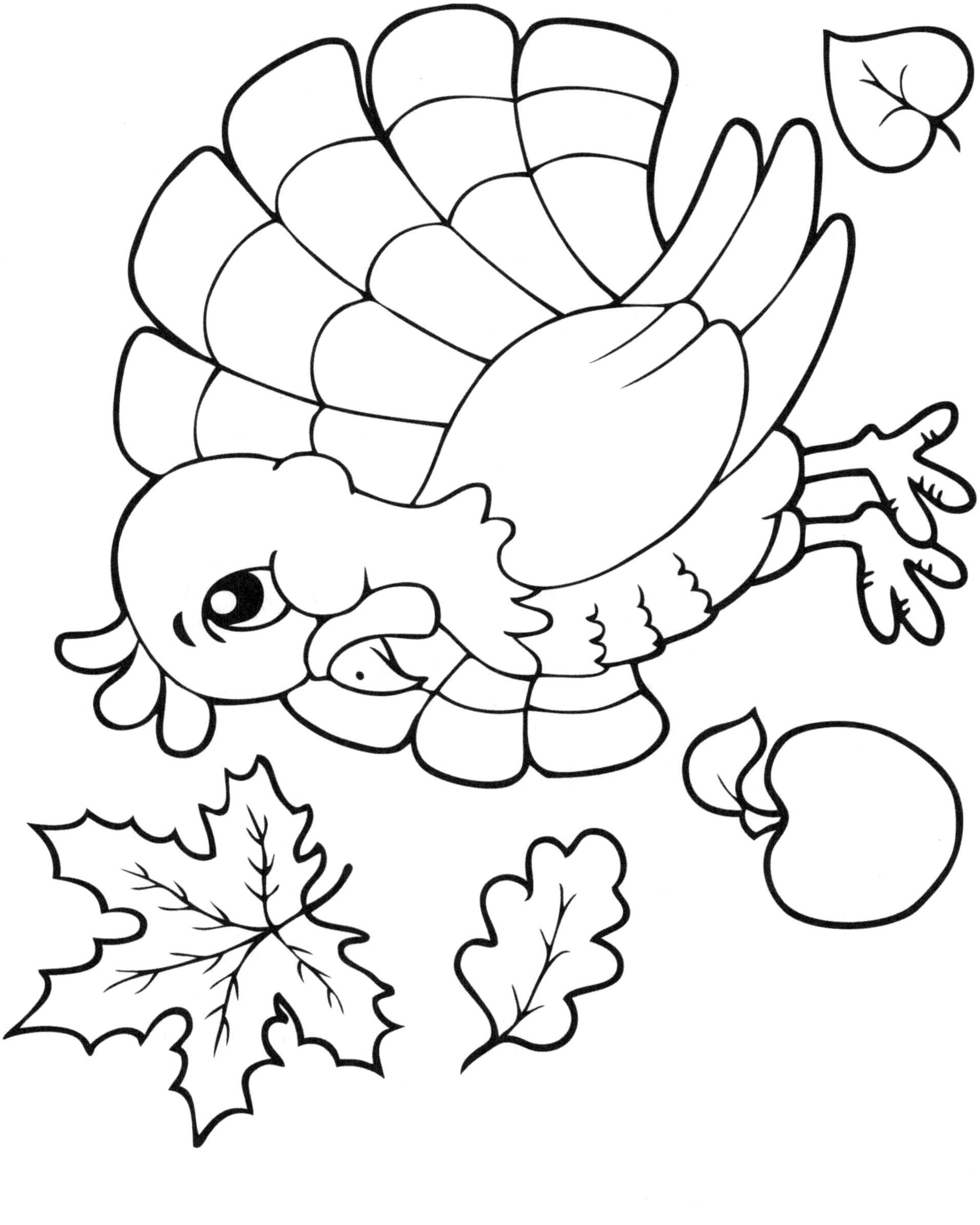

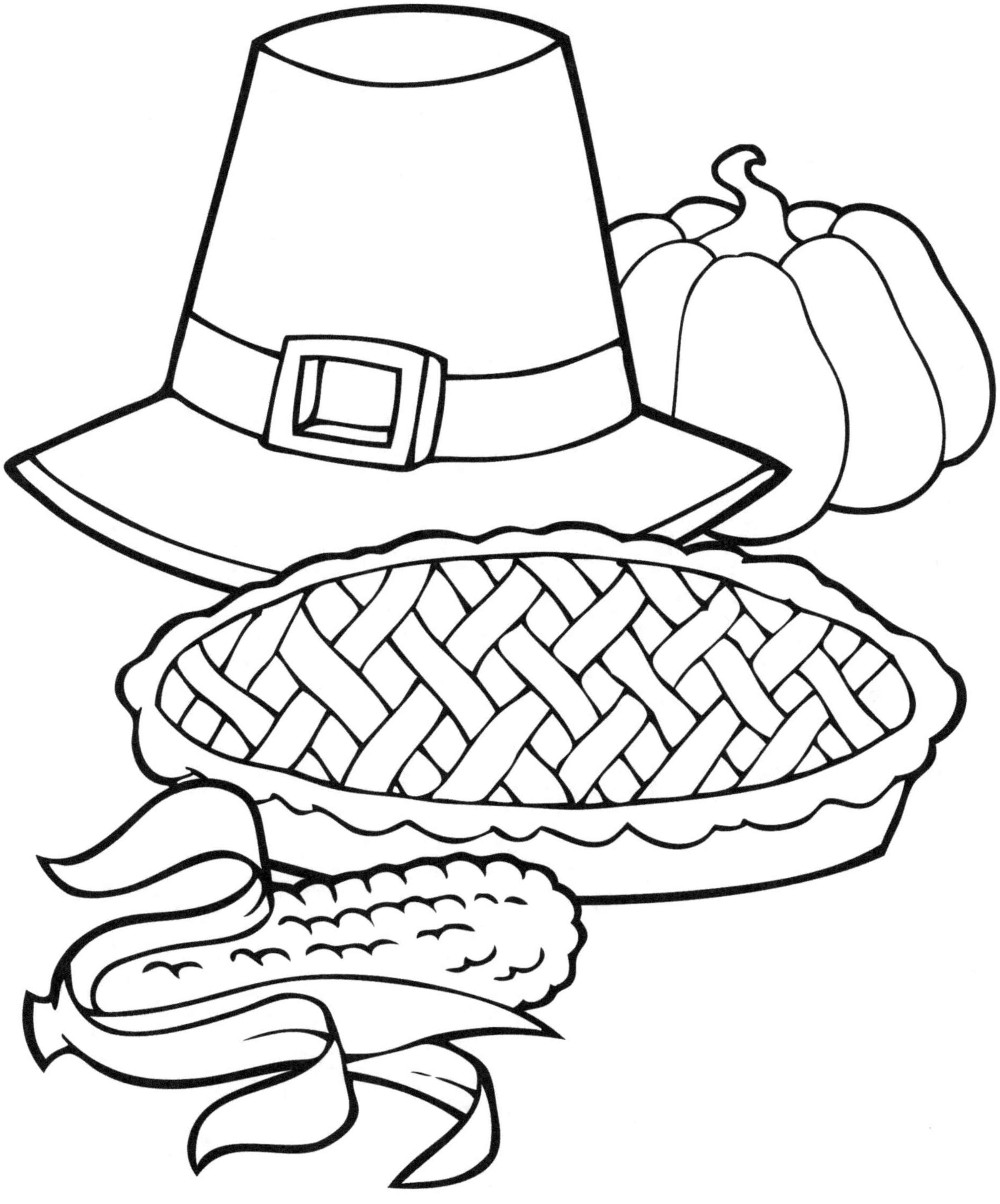

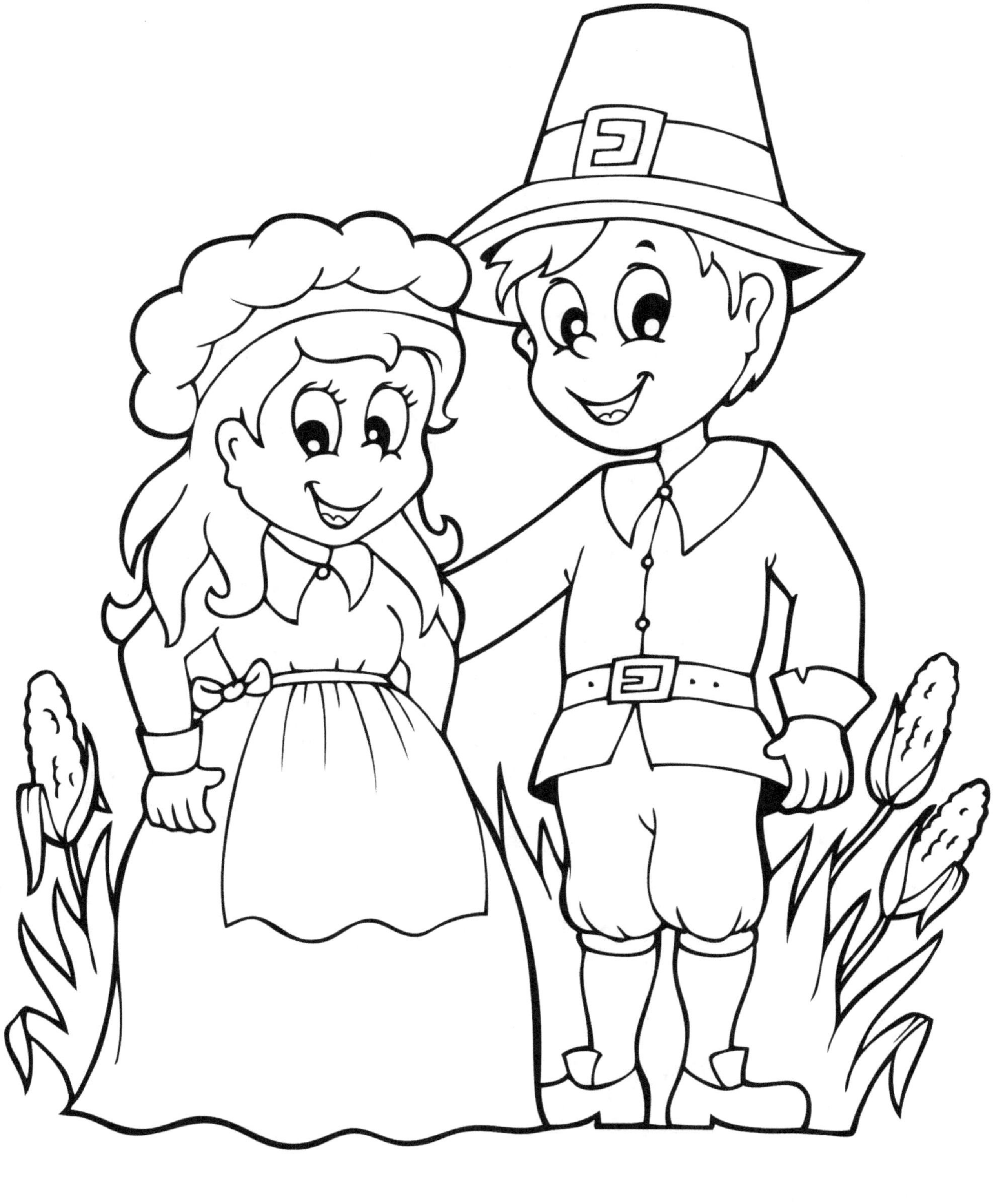

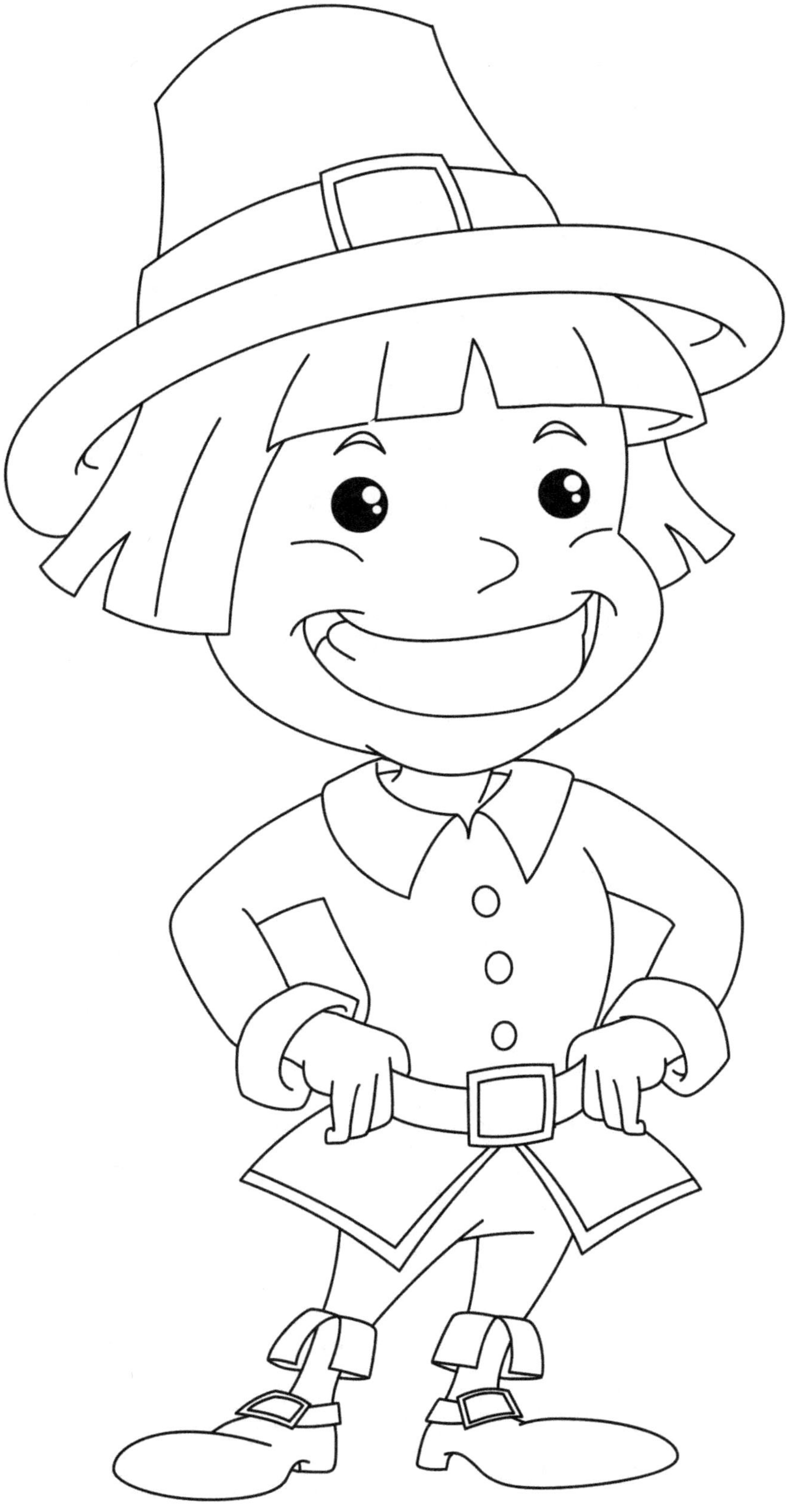

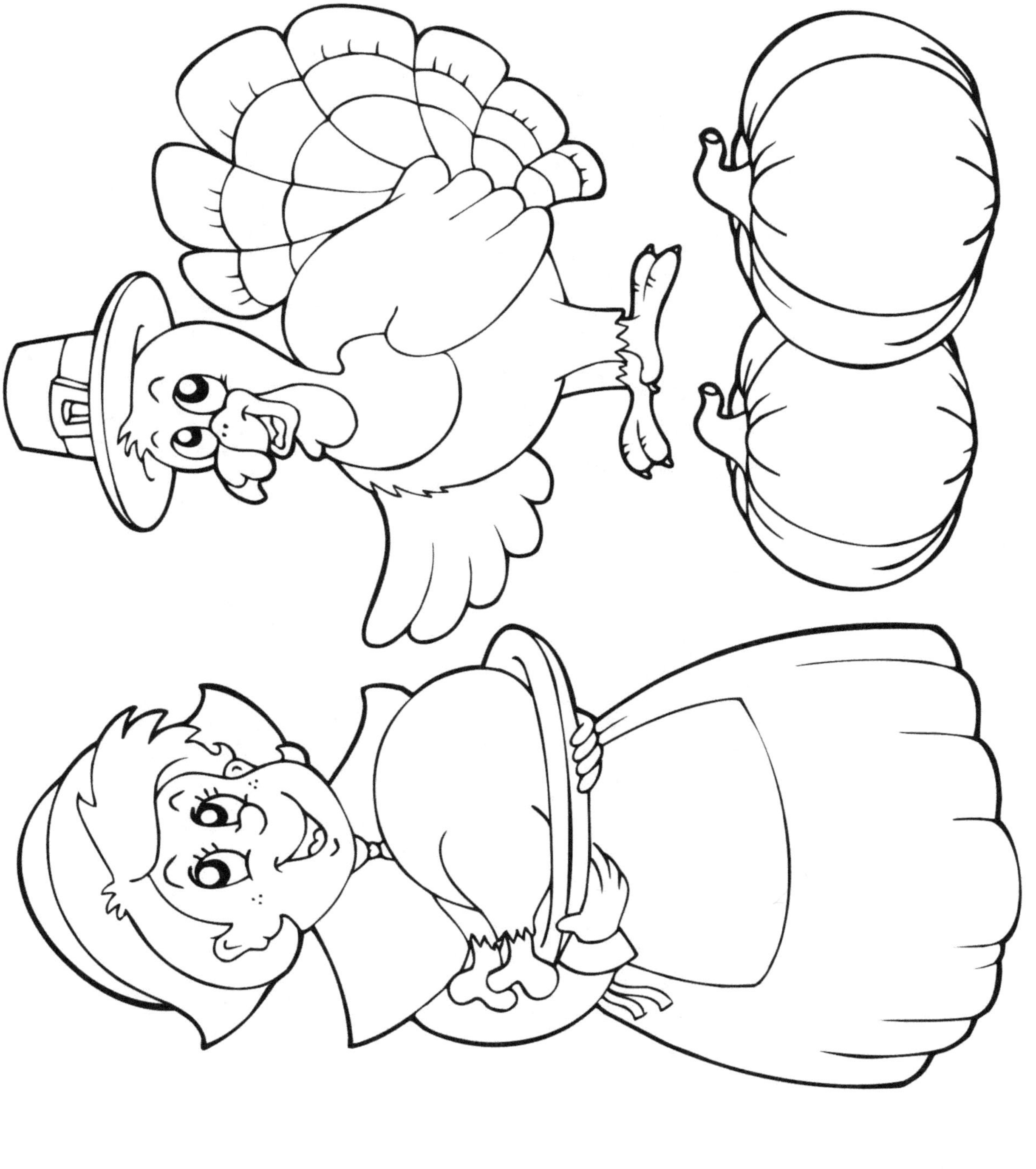

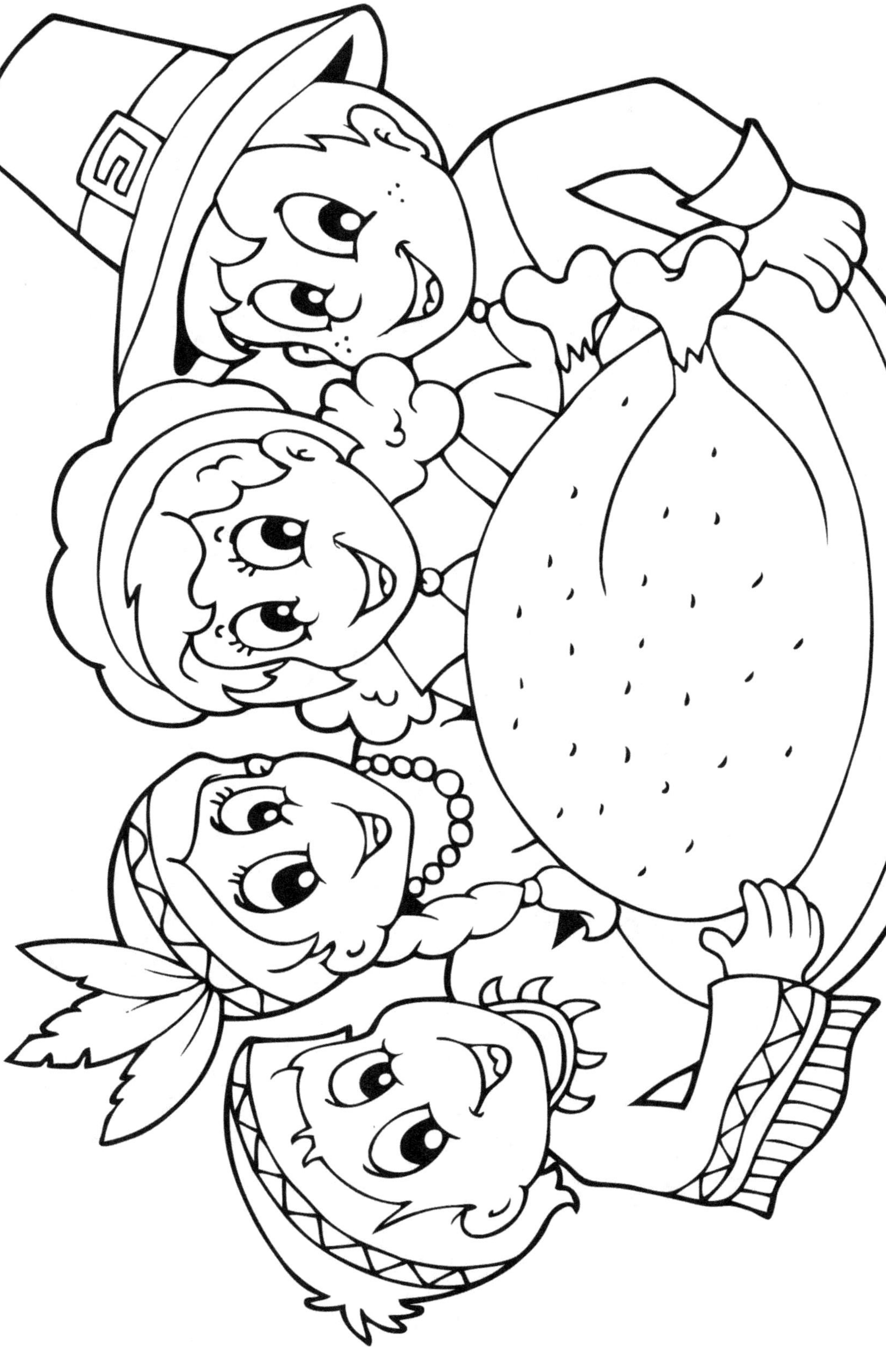

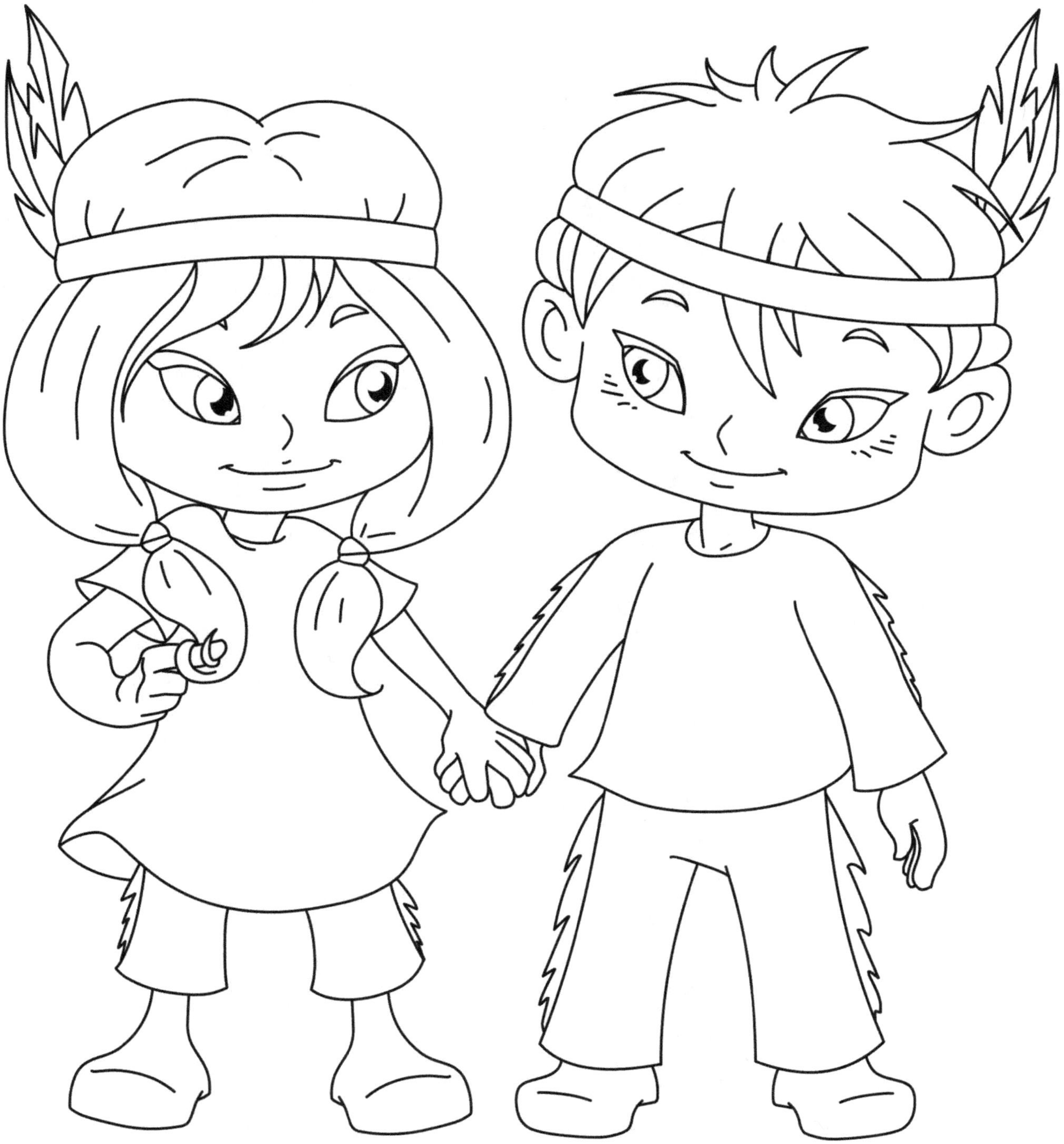

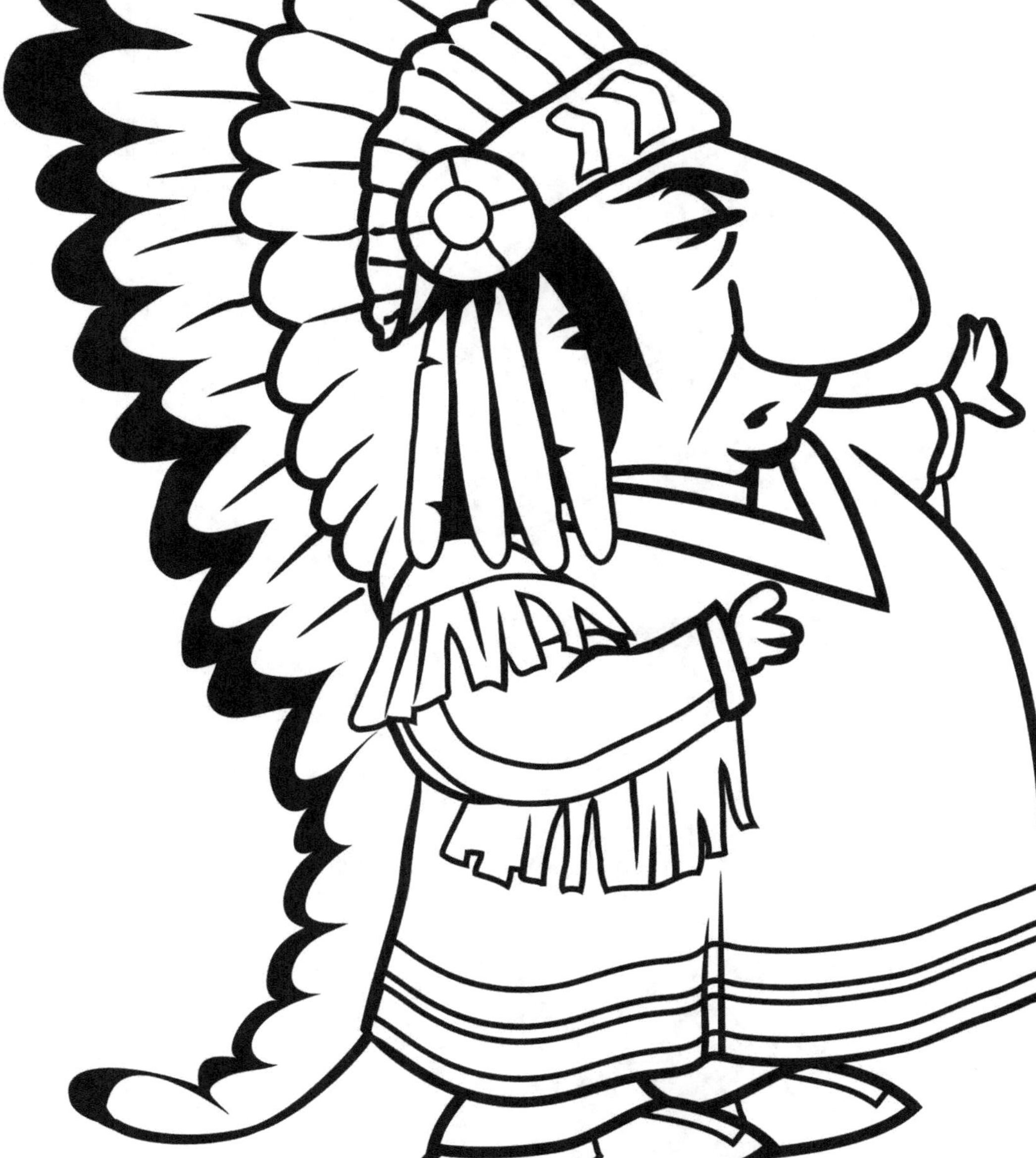

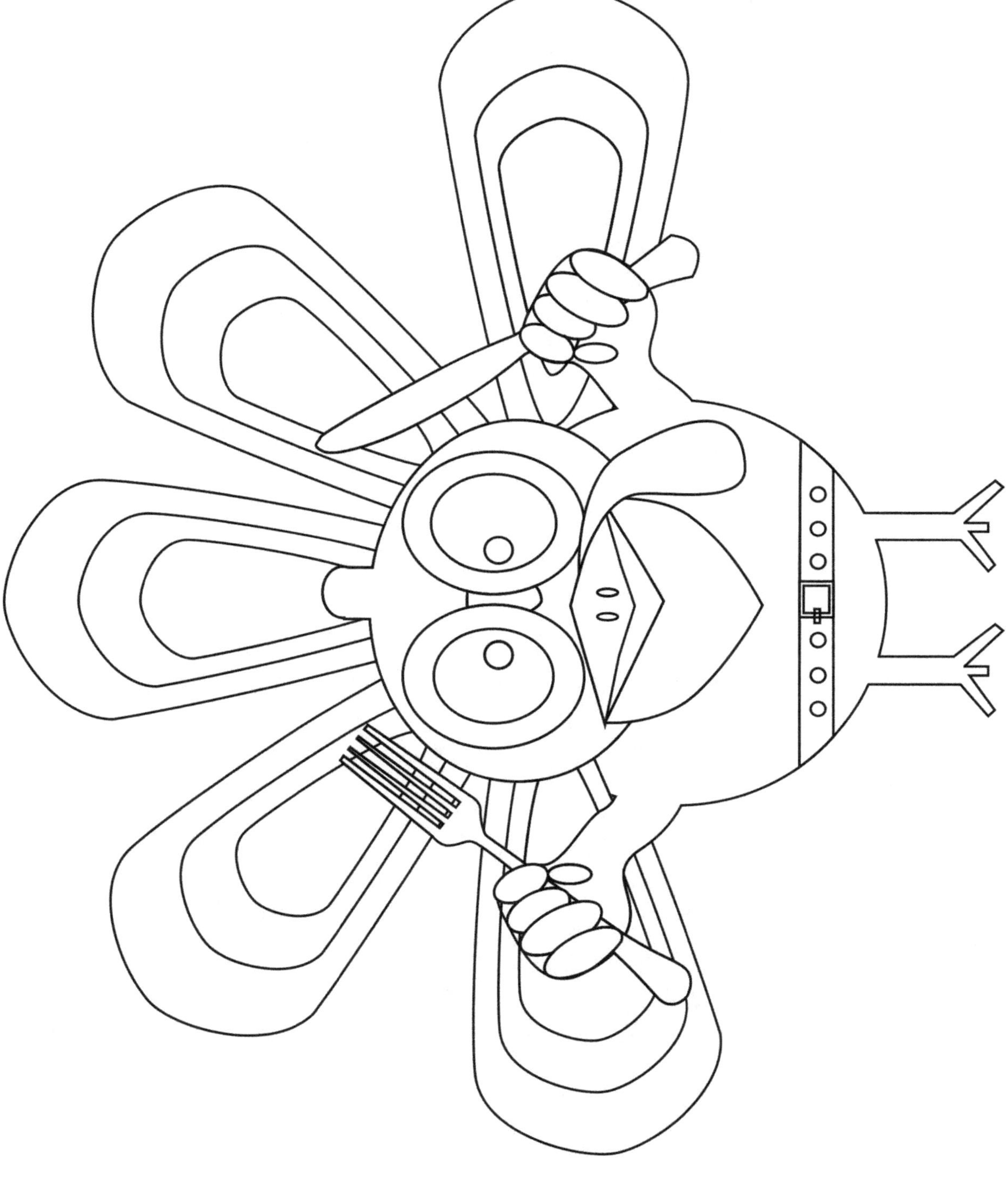

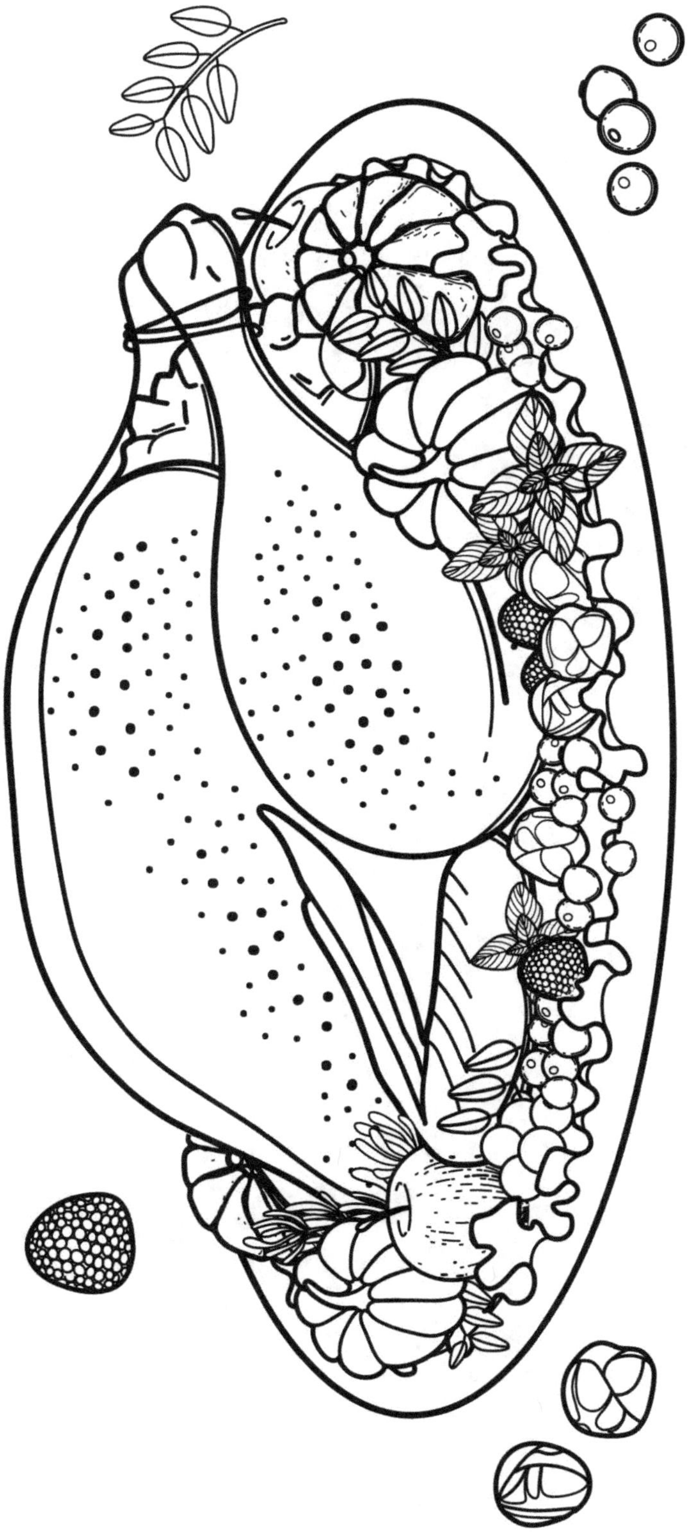

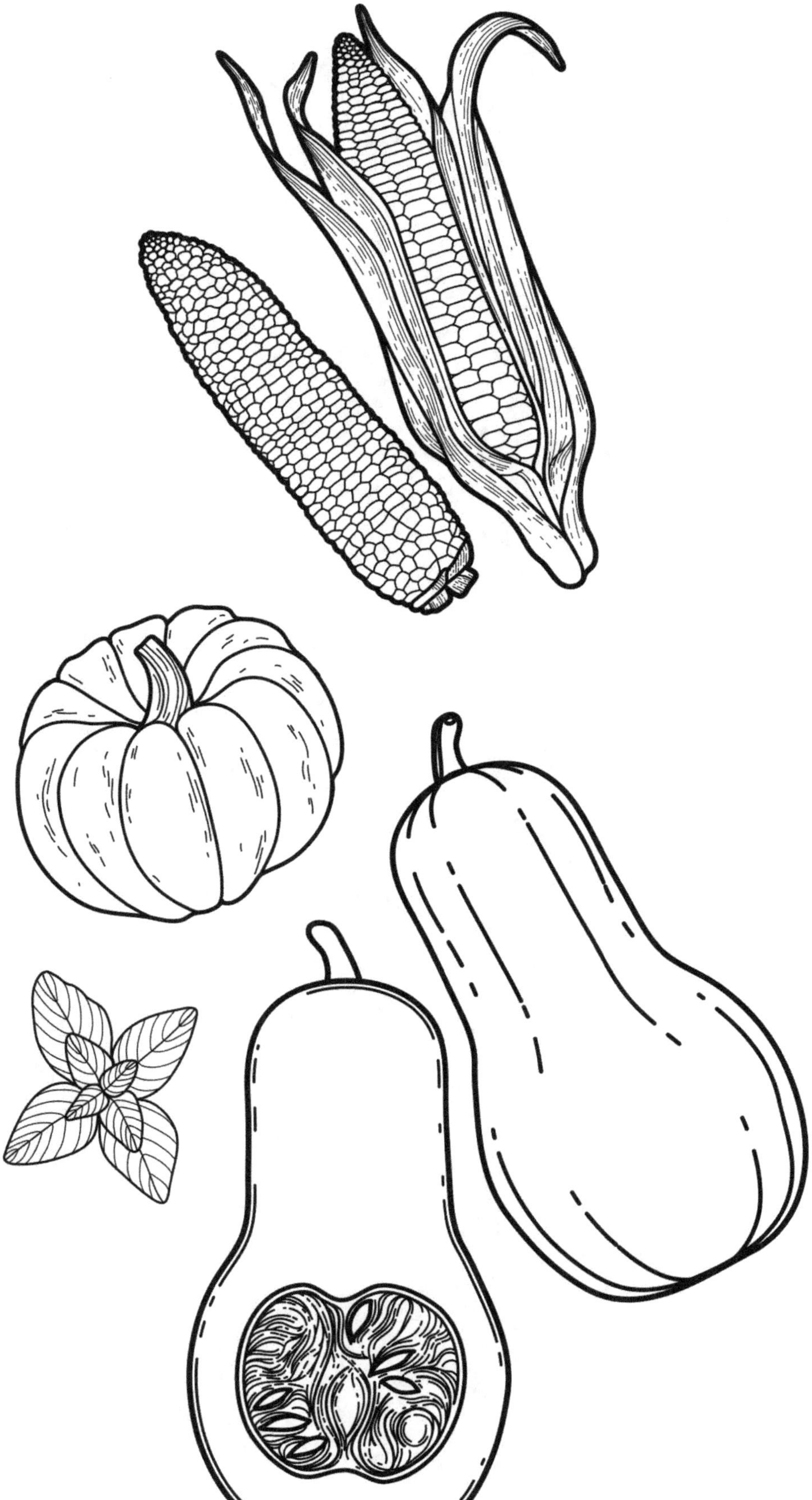

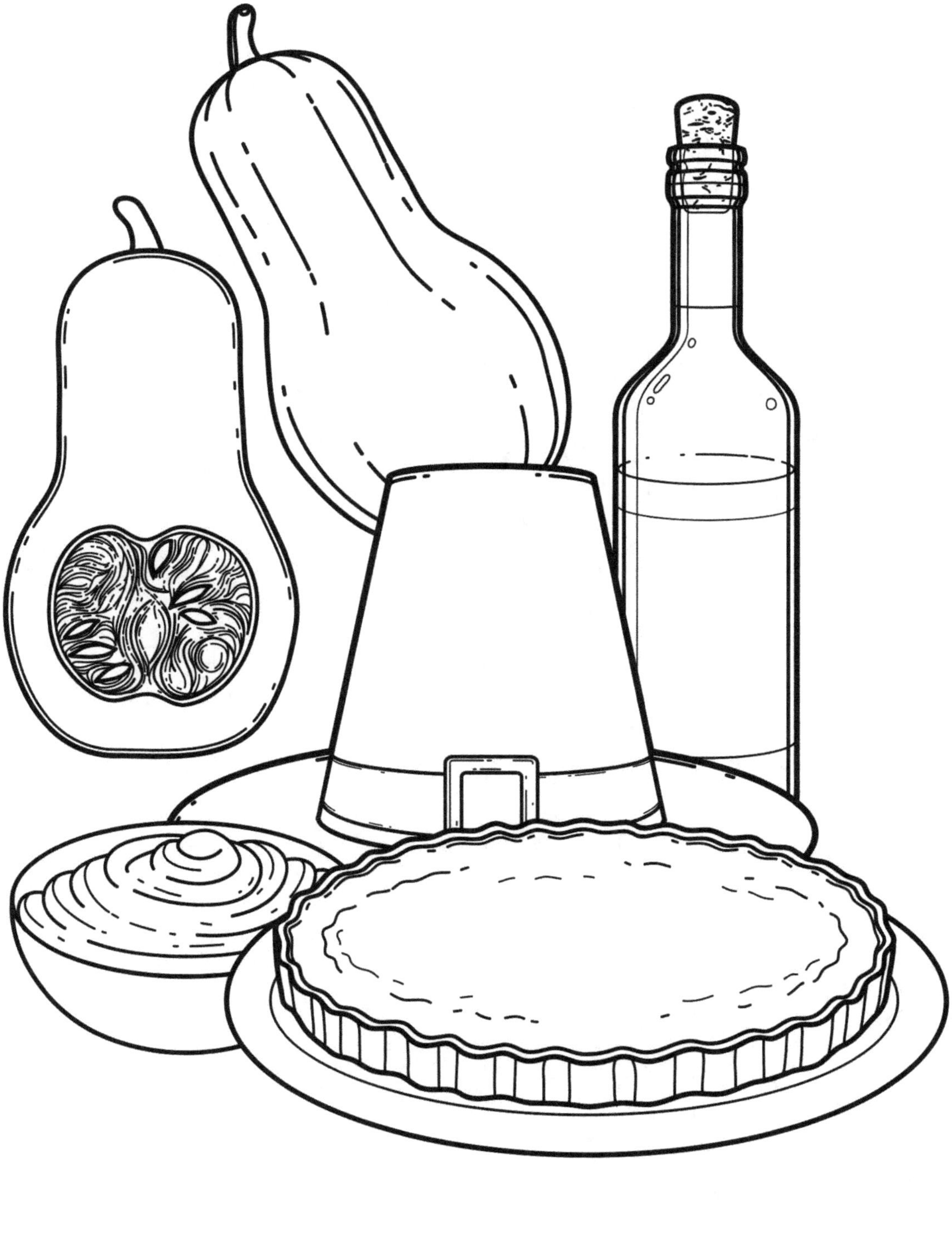

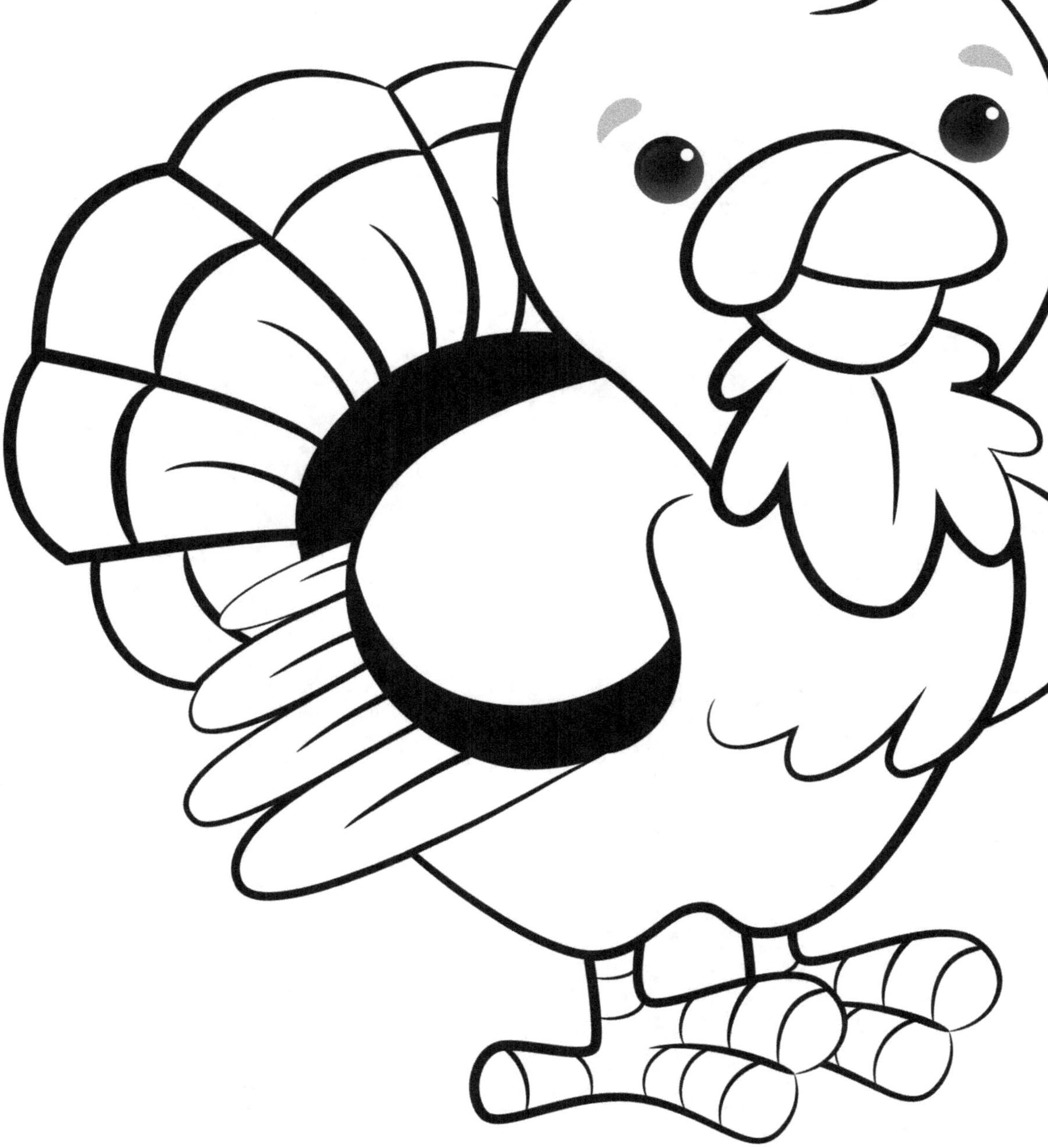

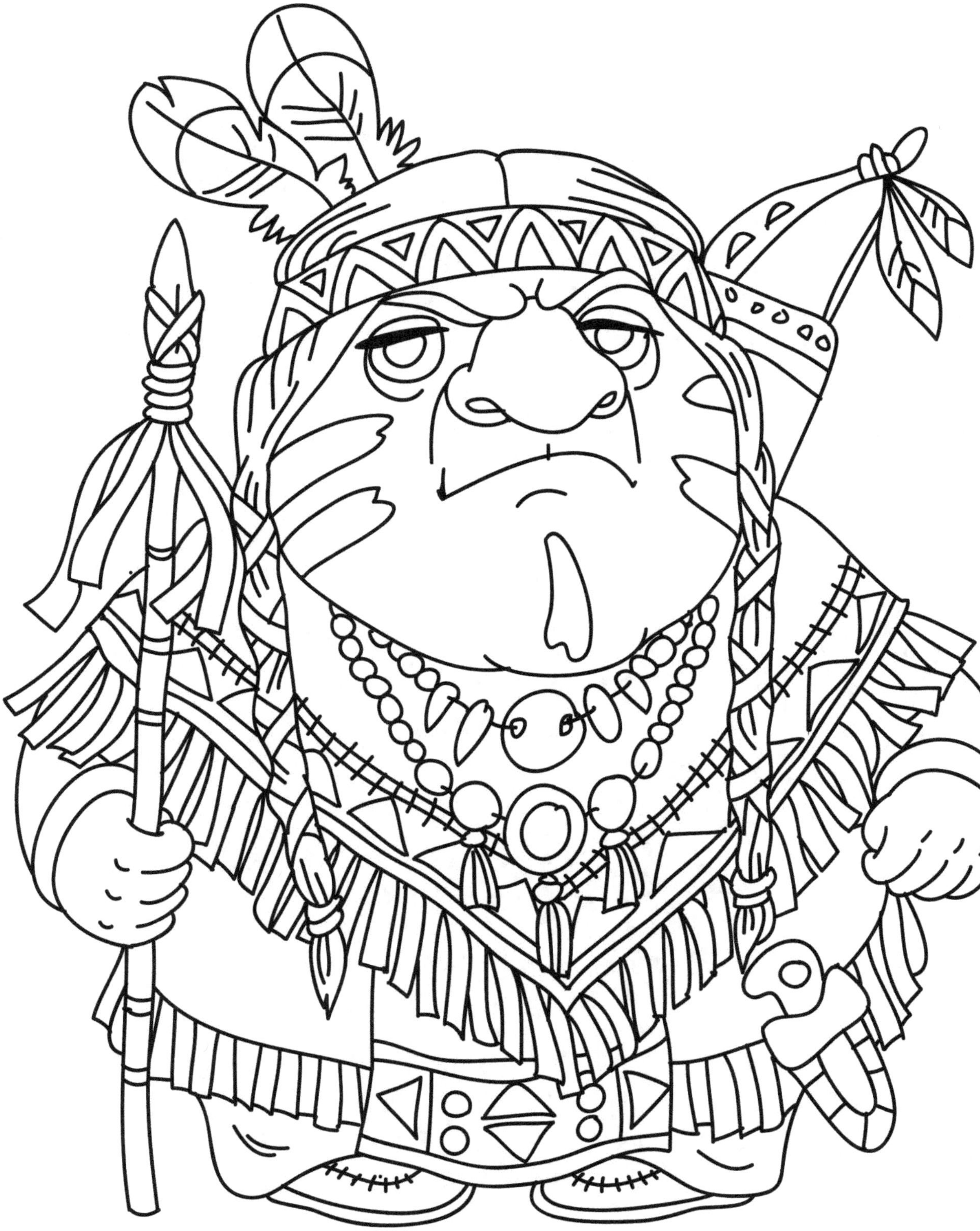

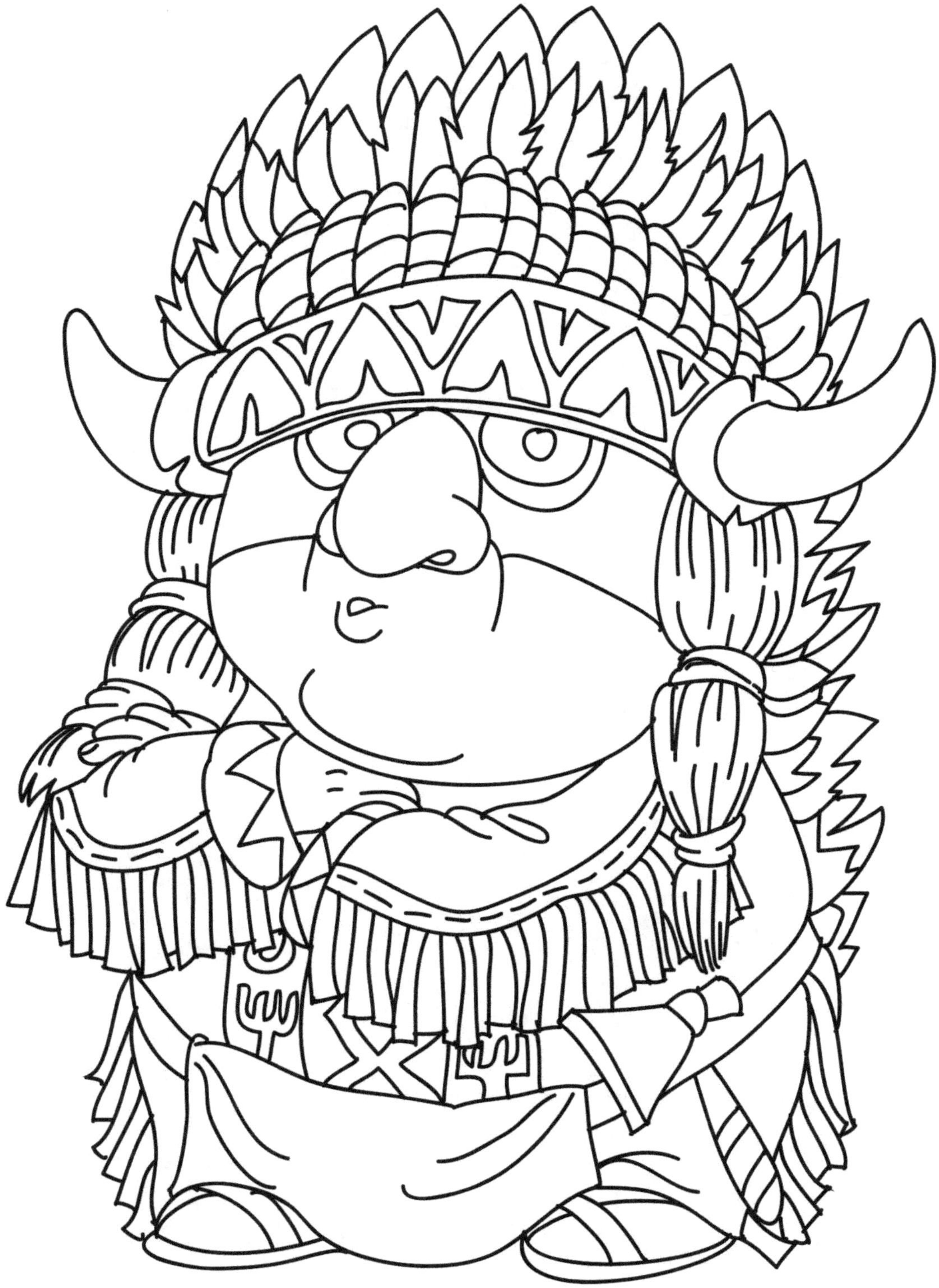

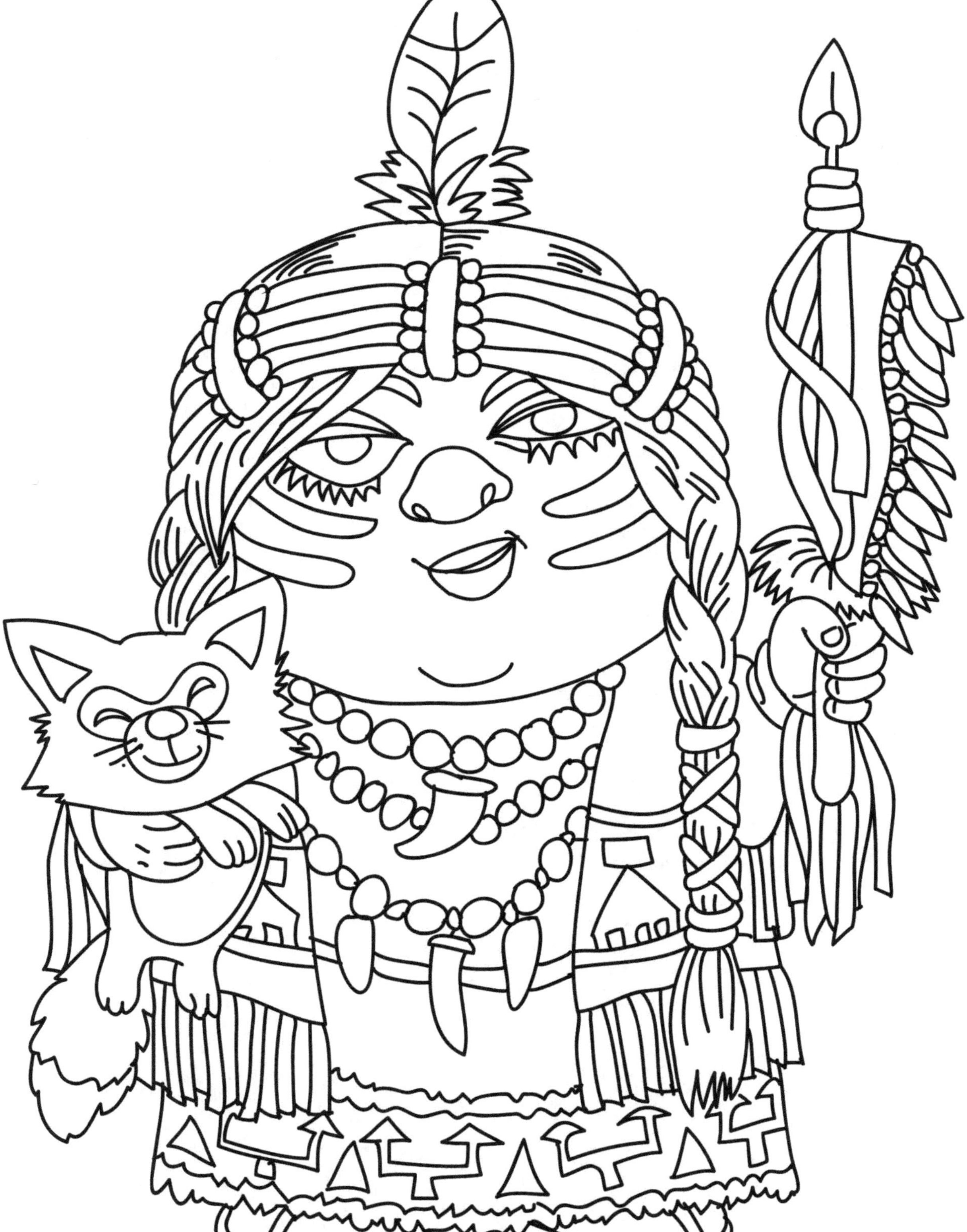

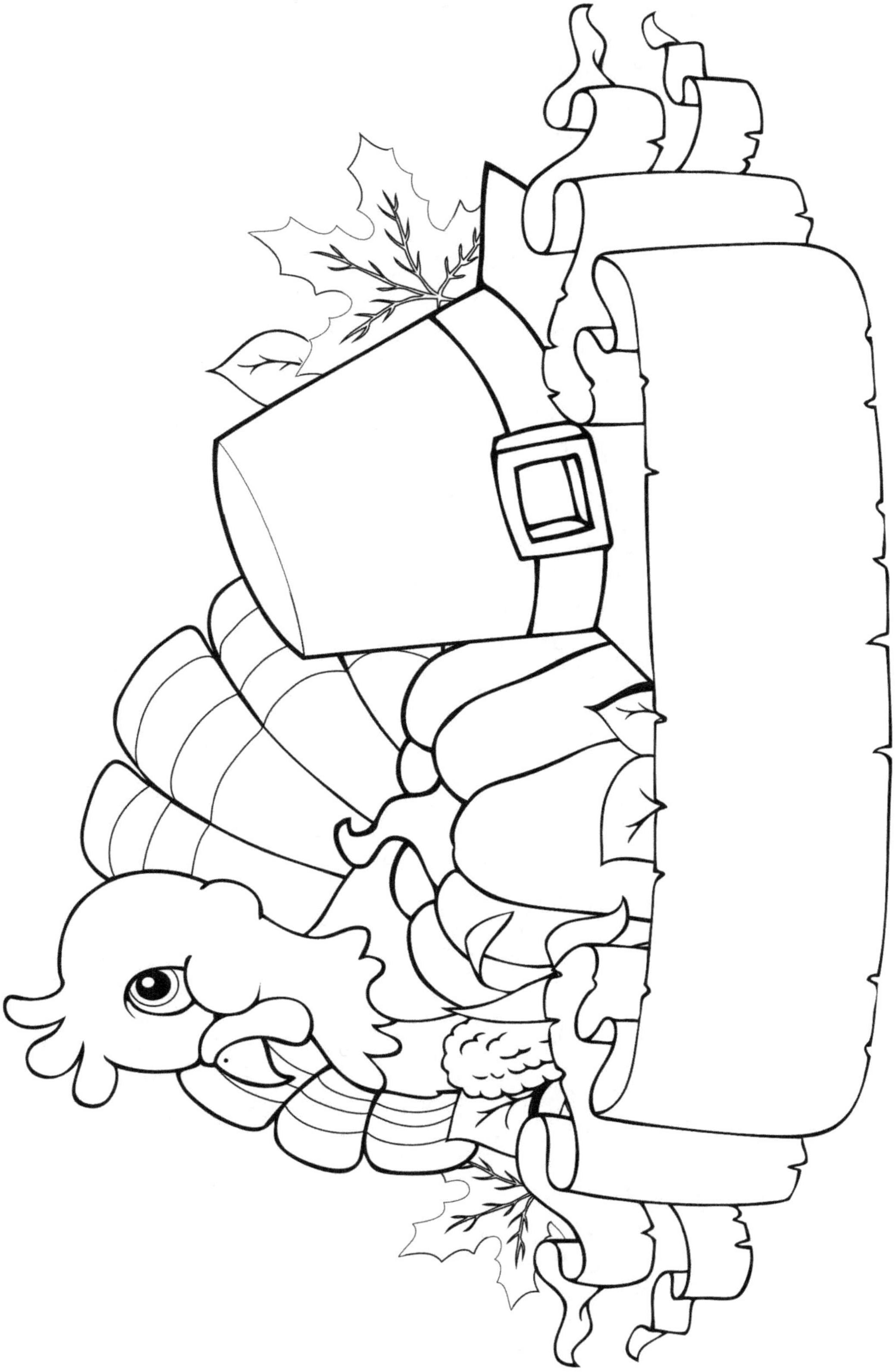

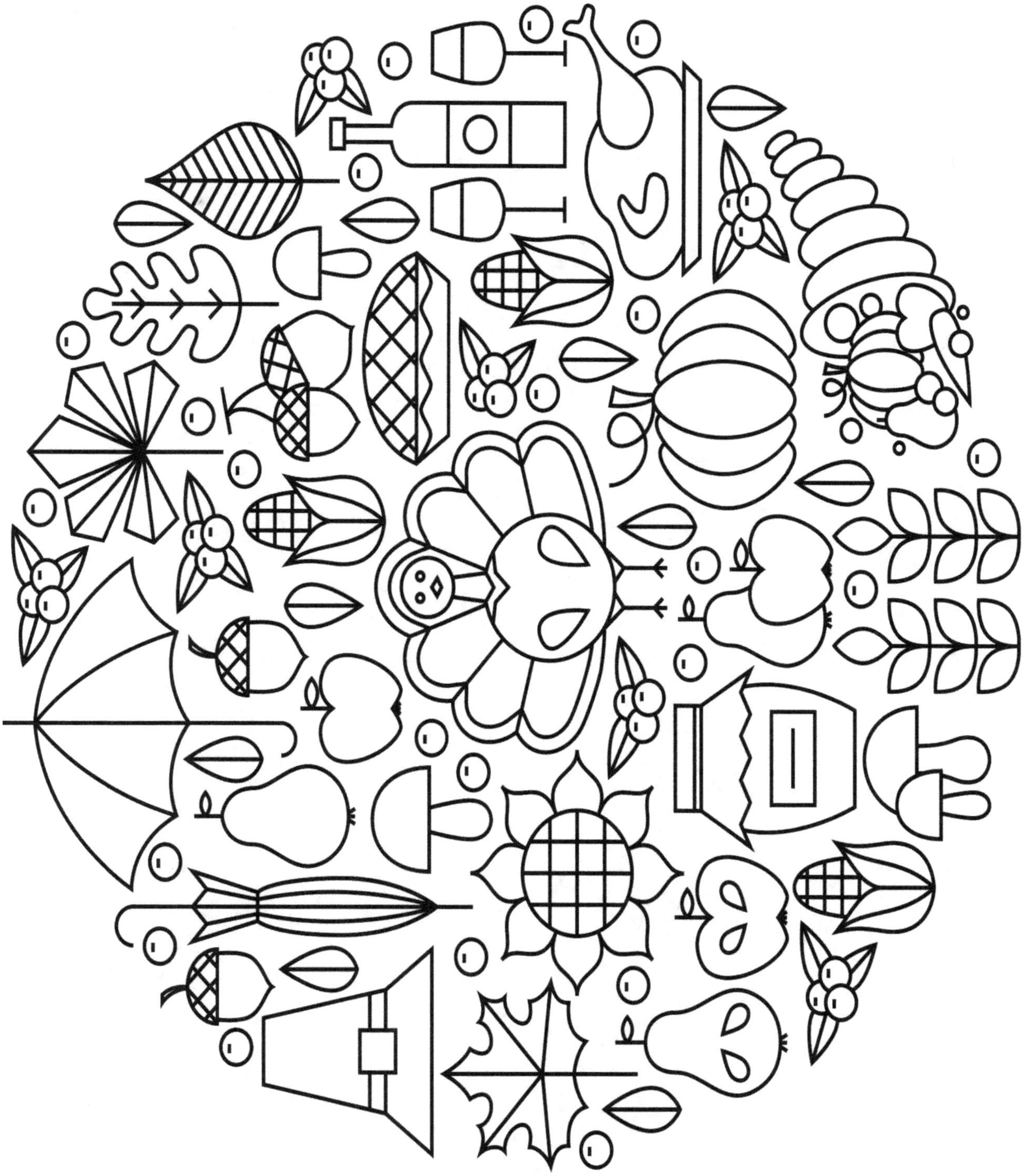

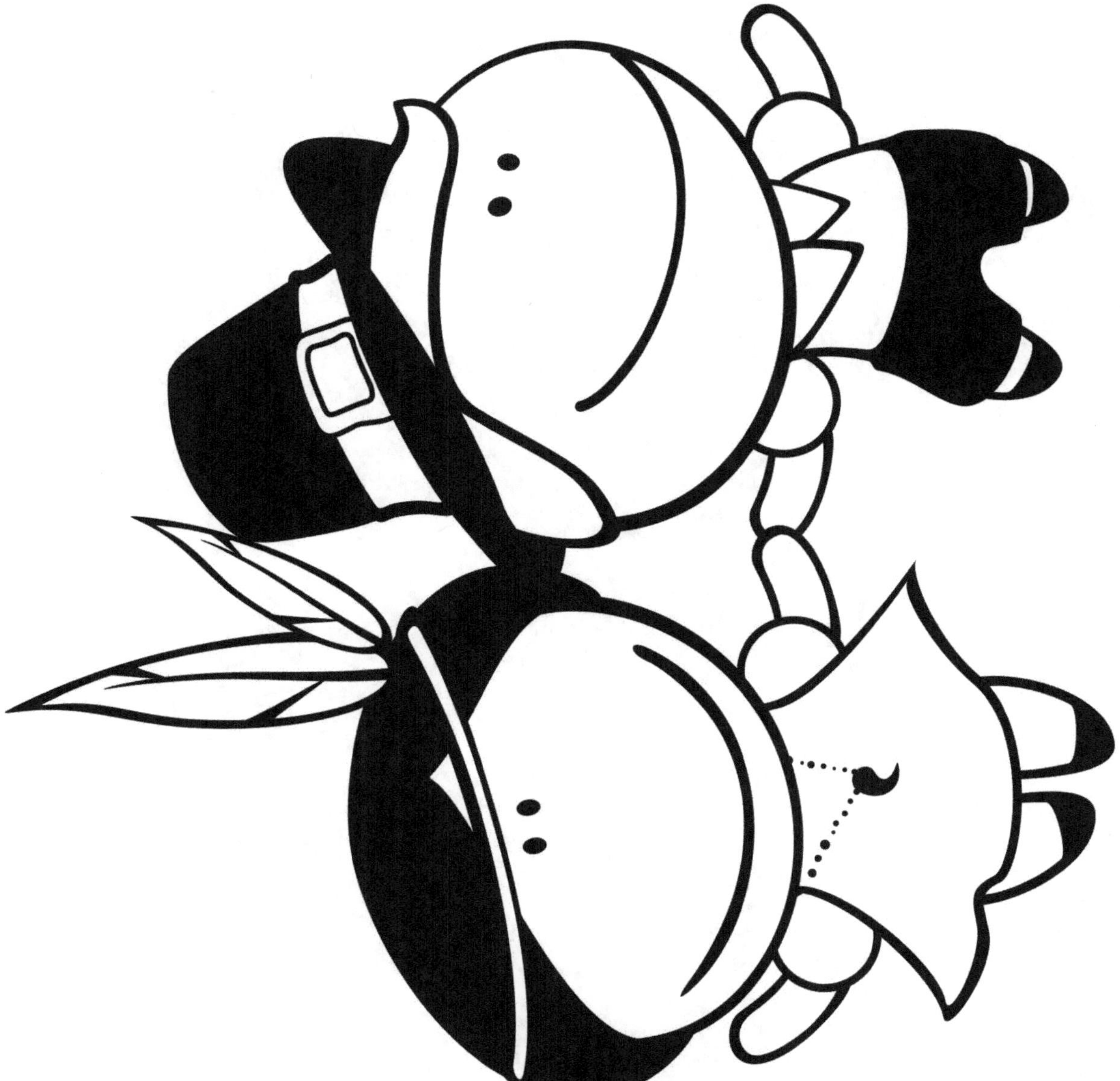

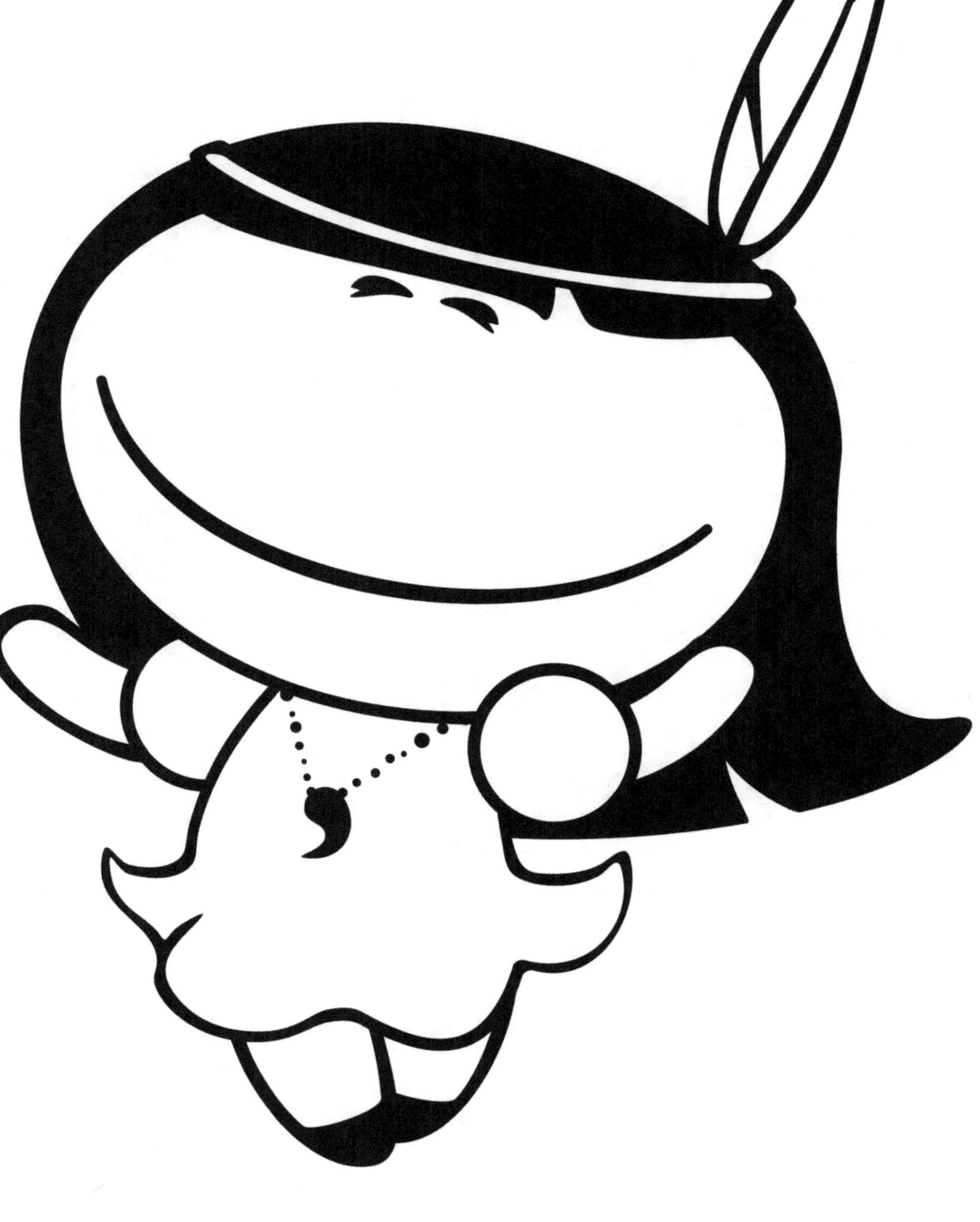

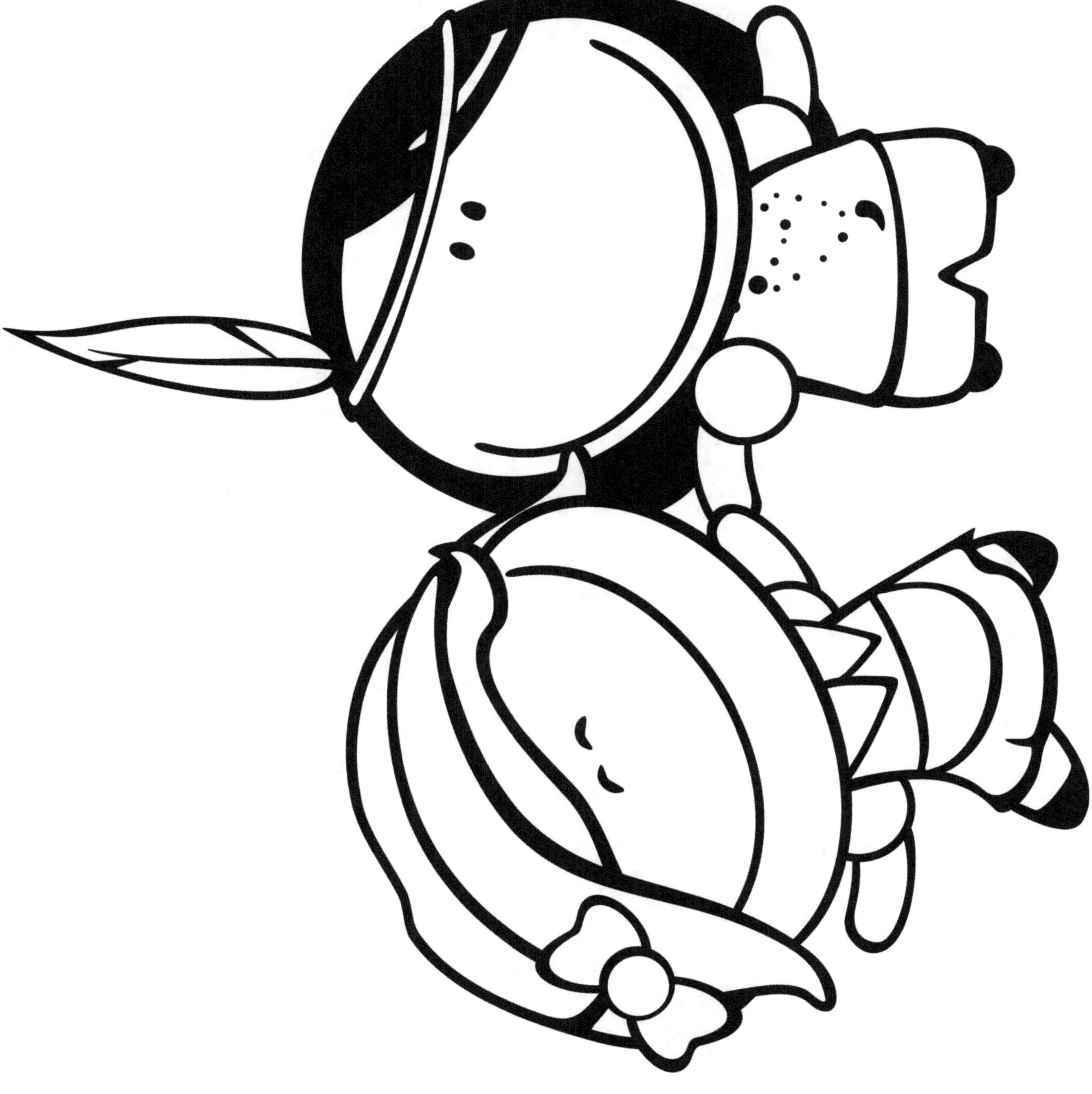

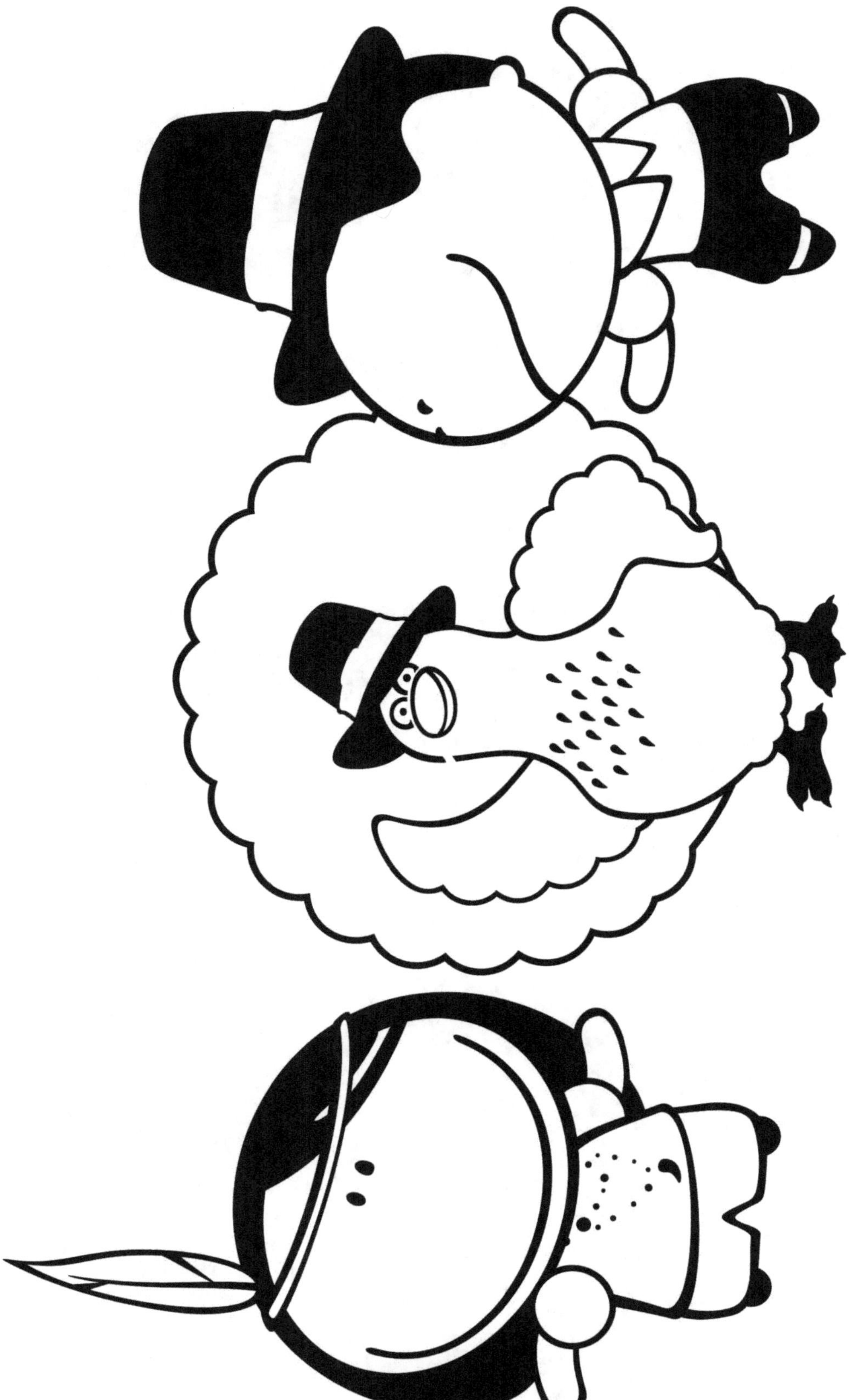

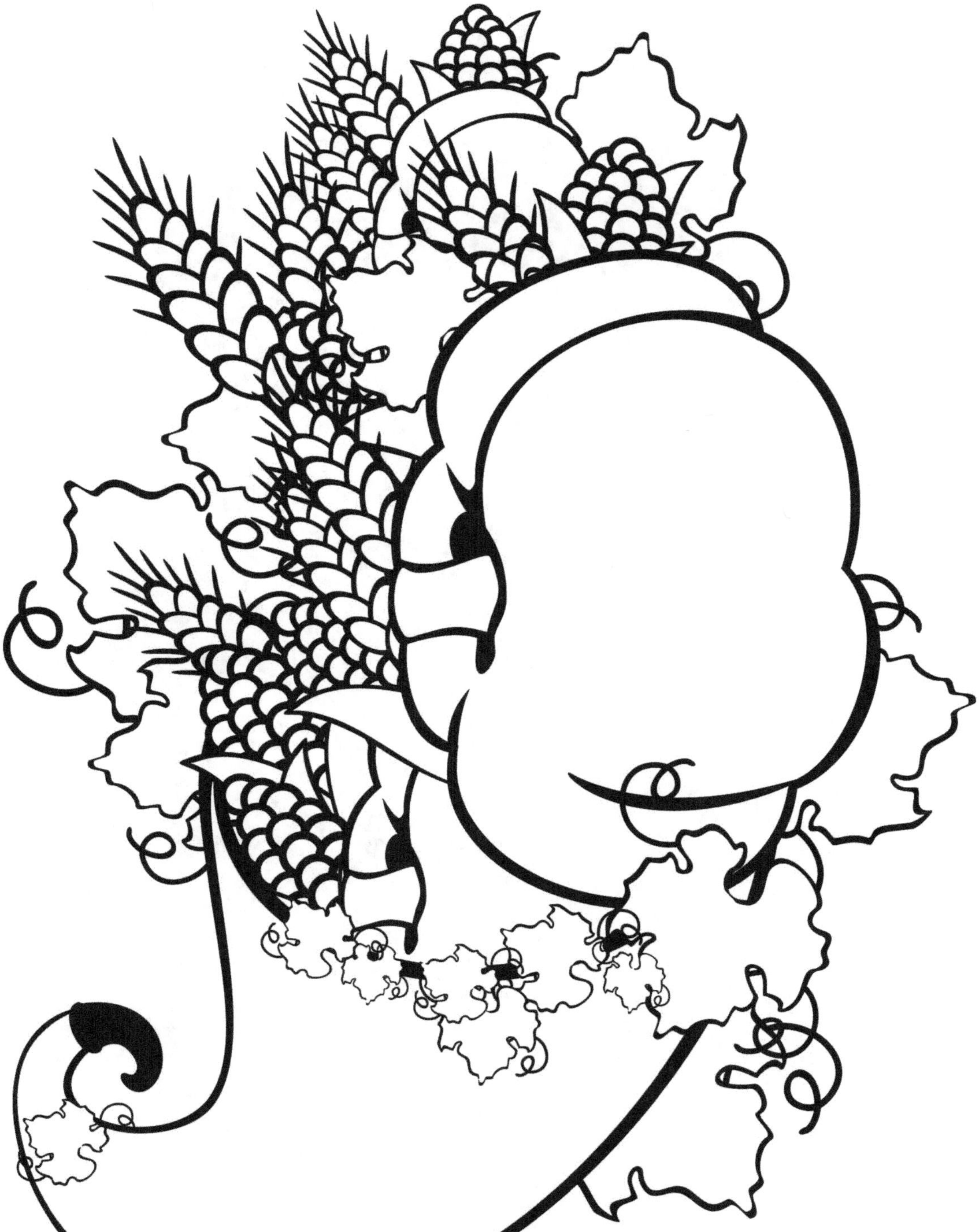

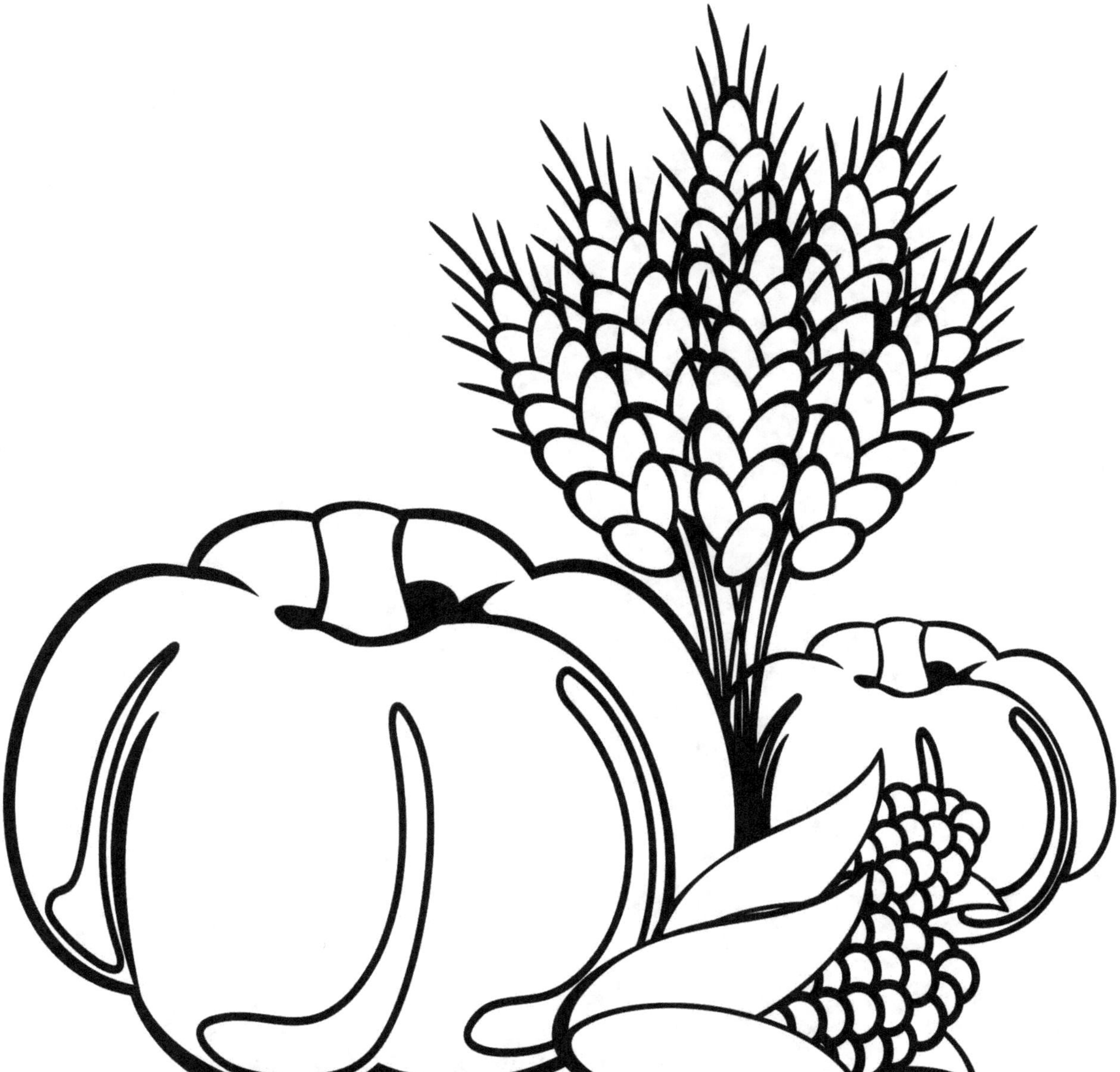

www.ingramcontent.com/pod-product-compliance
Lightning Source LLC
Chambersburg PA
CBHW062156220526
45470CB00009B/2844
* 9 7 8 1 9 7 9 6 9 8 1 1 5 *